Fat Old Woman in Las Vegas

Gambling, Dieting and Wicked Fun

Copyright

Dennis, Pat
Fat Old Woman in Las Vegas:
Gambling, Dieting & Wicked Fun
Summary: Memoir Travel
Cover Photograph: Donna Seline (Copyright ® 2014)
Cover Design: Pat Dennis/Marilyn Victor

Dedication

To Roy Roberts, my dad

Beginnings

My love affair with Las Vegas began twenty plus years ago, starting with a quickly arranged wedding and a silent protest. The nuptials were not mine, but the protest certainly belonged to me. The tacky city I envisioned Vegas to be held little interest. I'd long tired of hearing about it from relatives and friends.

No other city like it in the world!

All you can eat for $2.99

The women are topless but it's classy! It's really classy, no matter what my wife says!

For years, the glittering metropolis lured my family members like lemmings wearing sunglasses. Of my four siblings, only one was not interested in taking a chance with Lady Luck. He'd experienced firsthand the effects of my father's failed efforts at the track in Chicago. To this day that one sibling remains the smartest of us all to ever walk this earth. My other three siblings were born gamblers, just like Dad and me. The only difference was I hadn't yet come to that realization. Not even my ten-minute encounter with a card-playing con artist on the streets of New York City in the '70s proved that gambling and easy money could easily become a problem for me.

I was thirty-one, broke and living in the Big Apple attempting to gain fame and fortune as a playwright. My only income came from working as a temp for six bucks an hour. I barely covered my rent, much less food, transportation or my massive student loan debt. Most weekdays, I found myself hoofing to and from

1

my job, no matter where it was located on the island. I couldn't afford the subway fare.

Every Friday I hurriedly cashed my payroll check at the nearest currency exchange. If there were bills to pay, I'd buy a money order or two. Like most poor folk, I didn't bother with a bank account. The money I received for my labor disappeared almost as quickly as it hit my palms. It was little wonder that the opportunity to double a week's pay looked like a gift from God, instead of a prank by the devil.

I remember it clearly. At 5:00 p.m., the temperature hovered in the high eighties. The city was sweltering and angry. It took me only a few minutes to get from my temp assignment in an air-conditioned office building to the jam-packed sidewalk outside. With each step, I inhaled a mixture of grit, cab exhaust and the smell of a dozen Chinese takeouts. Living in NYC meant my mouth always tasted like metallic dust particles. In the tote bag I carried the cork soled platform high heels I wore at work. My feet were encased in sneakers for the long walk home. I'd taken off the padded-shoulder black polyester pantsuit jacket and carried it over my arm instead. My ratted, overly hairsprayed bouffant melted down my face and stuck to my cheap pancake makeup. I dreaded going back to my lonely studio apartment with its lack of air conditioning or a window fan.

As I turned the street corner, I saw a small crowd of half a dozen people gathered around a large cardboard box. On top were three playing cards, laid out in a horizontal row. Standing over the box was a sloppily dressed man. His smudged navy and white nylon tracksuit hung on his wiry frame. His opened jacket revealed a dirty white t-shirt. Two thick gold neck chains hung around his neck.

Sidling up next to me was an older gentleman in a threadbare suit. His face was the definition of a hangdog. The scent of mothballs tangoed with the smell of Old Spice aftershave. Hangdog became immersed at the spectacle that played out in front of us.

In Tracksuit's hand balanced a stack of currency. Tracksuit riffled through it, making one bill snap loudly against the next. He yelled, "Who's in? Ain't got all day. You're gonna win anyway. Might as well double your money sooner rather than later. Who's in?"

A few onlookers scuffled away. Others stayed and giggled. Hangdog reached into his pocket and pulled out three twenty-dollar bills.

Tracksuit looked skeptical. "You sure, Grandpa? Can you even see the cards?" His hand gestured at the box top.

What Hangdog said next surprised me, but I assumed he'd been embarrassed by the punk. He barked back, "Fuck you, asshole. Don't give me any lip. I'm in."

He handed Tracksuit the sixty bucks.

I still had no idea what was going to actually happen. During the months I had been in the city, I'd occasionally walked by card games being played on the streets. I never stopped to watch. They held no interest for me. I'd yet to write mysteries or research con artists for plot elements. Somehow, I had avoided seeing Paul Newman in *The Sting*.

I was the perfect, innocent mark, just ripe for the taking.

Tracksuit flipped the three crimped cards face up. There were two black cards, one a five of spades and the other a five of clubs. In the middle was a red card, the Queen of Diamonds.

He turned the cards over and started switching them back and forth between his hands. He instructed in a firm voice, "Remember to look for the red queen. Always look for the red queen. Keep your eyes on the red." After seven or eight switches of the cards he laid the cards in a horizontal row, next to each other.

The old guy pointed his veiny finger at the card in the middle and said, "That one."

Tracksuit turned it over. His mouth fell open. "Damn it," he replied before regaining his composure. "You're good, old man."

Hangdog had chosen correctly. He'd doubled his money. But instead of walking away, he let it ride. He won again. I quickly calculated his earnings. Hangdog was $240.00 richer.

When asked if he wanted to try a third time, Hangdog shook his head. "I'm not an idiot," he responded walking away, stuffing his newly earned fortune into his pocket.

The next participant, a busty young gum-chewing bimbo, waved a few bucks in the air.

"You sure sweetie?" Tracksuit asked as he took her money from her hand. Bimbo quickly lost the ten bucks. She pouted and then used the F word three times before swaying away.

It hadn't surprised me Bimbo lost. She hadn't paid close enough attention to the cards. It was obvious which was the red queen, the one she should have chosen. If she'd been using her eyes to focus, rather than to check out her manicure, she would have known it was the card on the right.

I had no choice but to play the game. I only hesitated for the briefest of moments. What was I planning on doing? I needed every single cent in my pocketbook. A demonic impulse reminded me ... I wanted more. In every area of my life, I wanted more. I needed more.

I knew I was smart like Hangdog. I could do what he did. More importantly, I wasn't as stupid as Bimbo. I could win at this. For the first time since I'd come to New York three months earlier, I'd have money to spare. I could put the money on my already overdue phone bill. I could go out to dinner. I missed dinner. I subsisted on breakfast food served at any time of the day. I devoured cereal like a frat boy.

I rummaged around in my purse. I wasn't foolish enough to pull out my hunk of cash on the street, just part of it. I carefully counted out one hundred dollars.

True, that amount was scheduled to go into my rent jar back at my apartment. But if I could put two hundred dollars in the empty Jiffy Peanut Butter jar instead, my future would be so much brighter. Maybe I could win three hundred bucks from this sucker.

But what happens, if I lose?

I stopped that thought from going any further. I wouldn't lose. It was time for my luck to change. I needed to believe in myself again. My entire life I'd been told I was too negative. Living in New York had only increased my pessimism. I needed to try something new and rather alien to me ... the power of positive thinking.

"Who's next? Who wants to double their ..." Tracksuit stopped mid-sentence as I waved a bit of greenery. He grabbed the money from my hand, not bothering to ask if I was sure I wanted to play.

He switched the cards back and forth on the box top as he yelped, "Keep your eyes on the red card. Keep your eyes on the red queen of diamonds. Always look for the red. Remember the red ...,"

He was wasting his breath. I didn't need to be reminded.

My brow furrowed as I concentrated on every movement of his hands. When he'd finished laying the last card down, I smiled a tiny smile. It was all too easy. Just like taking candy from a baby-faced thug.

I pointed at the three cards lying side by side and then carefully pointed at the one on the far side with my index finger. I announced, "The one on the left."

Tracksuit flipped over the card. I had chosen the five of spades.

My mouth dropped open. My throat turned into sand. I managed to garble out loud, "No way. No fucking way. I couldn't have lost. It couldn't have been ..."

"Shut the fuck up," Tracksuit sneered. "You lost fair and square. Get outta here."

5

Tracksuit's neck muscles tightened. The look of being a perpetual dope transformed into that of an angry, vengeful man.

I started again. "I want my money... I couldn't have lost ... You tricked me ... You . . ."

The small crowd encircling tittered at my desperation. I continued to stammer to the point of hyperventilation. The crowd grew even larger and more pleased. There's nothing a New Yorker likes more than waiting for someone to jump off the edge of a building.

"I, I, I . . ." I said, not able to put a coherent sentence together.

"Lady, shut the fuck up. The cops will hear you," a gravelly voice from behind whispered in my ear.

I recognized the scent. I turned my head. It was Hangdog. He nodded at Tracksuit who quickly gathered up his cards. Tracksuit kicked over the cardboard box and fled to the East. So did Hangdog. Immediately, I knew they were running off to meet The Bimbo, who was smarter than I was after all.

I had been had. Tricked. Conned. Screwed. There was absolutely no way I could replace the money I'd just lost. I'd long since tapped out any possibilities of future loans from family or friends.

Standing on that street corner, feeling like the Greenwich Village Idiot, I vowed to never gamble again. Ever. And except for a few lottery tickets here and there, I didn't. Not until I hit Las Vegas, decades later and my dormant gambling gene became activated.

∞

It wasn't surprising that one of my brothers chose Nevada to be his home. The day he retired as a railroad switchman in the Midwest, he drove to the desert. His thick, winter gloves and thicker coat were discarded for a security guard uniform at The Showboat on Boulder

Highway. He'd never been happier or more content. Another brother would visit Vegas three or four times a year. He'd brag about cheap food and amazing shows. Translation? All-you-can-eat buffets and all-you-can-stare-at boobs. It didn't get better than that for a guy from the South Side of Chicago. Even my sister seemed to love Sin City.

The few times my siblings and I gathered together as adults, if Mom wasn't around, the only stories shared were about their latest gambling junket.

I'd sit there judgmentally clinching my jaw and rolling my eyes. Why would any one choose the exact same place to visit, year after year? Didn't they realize there were more exciting places to visit? Exotic locales? Like Paris? Or London? Even Greenland would be more interesting than a smoke filled casino and a cheesy hotel room decorated to look like Paris on a bad day.

I'd try to block out their stories of inexpensive breakfasts or Sammy Davis Jr. sightings. My male siblings would marvel how classy the shows were, even if the women were half naked. There was nothing scandalous about the shows at all. Nothing. Why *Nudes on Ice* could easily be considered family entertainment, something you could proudly have your wife attend. The wives would look embarrassed and hide behind giggles and blushes.

Meanwhile, I sat there silently vowing to never, ever travel to Las Vegas. If I wanted to see a woman's breasts, I'd just look in a mirror. And if I wanted to see a female with feathers resting on her head, I'd buy a parrot.

It wasn't until I was past the age of forty that I caught the Vegas virus.

A beloved family member's call to duty presented very few options for a spur of the moment wedding venue. The reception, held at Caesar's Palace in Las Vegas, was an elegant occasion. The bride and groom paraded through the casino under a moving military processional of crossed swords. A few rounds of applause could be heard from bystanders, but mostly there were the sounds of coins slapping into metal trays.

The wedding reception was in an elaborate private dining room serviced by stiff waiters in tuxedos. Their hands, donned in starched, white gloves, carefully placed china plates in front of us. At an appropriate time during the first course, the stained glass domed ceiling slid open to reveal a black, star-filled Nevada sky. Perhaps it was this experience … so far beyond my sibling's description of $3.99 buffets … that awakened the gambling DNA in me.

Oh, and the fact that I almost won a thousand dollars the day after the wedding, may have contributed to my reawakened yearnings as well.

As any seasoned gambler will tell you, it's the almost wins that get you hooked every single time.

∞

The day after the wedding I had a few hours to kill before my husband and I were to check out of our hotel. I strolled around the casino with a large paper bucket partially filled with quarters. Ticket-in, ticket-out slot machines had yet to be invented.

My fingertips were black with coin grime. I slid quarters one at time into one machine after another. I walked down the aisle and dropped one quarter into a slot, pulled the lever, and moved onto the next. If I heard any dinging I turned swiftly around to see what I'd won. Usually, it was a quarter, which I'd lose on the very next pull of the lever.

I had forty dollars in quarters to lose before I left Vegas and went home to my real life … that of a boring, frugal housewife slash small time comedian slash even smaller time writer.

Until that trip, I was a coupon cutting, thrift store shopping, cheap-as-dirt gal. But, because I was in Sin

City, nothing I did actually mattered, right? Besides, to this day, I have this rule about being on a vacation, and that is no rules are allowed. I drink what I want to drink, eat what I want to eat, flirt with whomever I want to, and then at the end, I come back to the grim reality of calorie counting, liquor restrictions, penny counting and a medieval-like monogamous role as dutiful wife.

I'd adopted the 'what happens in Vegas, stays in Vegas' attitude way before the slogan was popularized by an ad campaign. What is a vacation for if not to take a break from everything in your life that makes you tense? And when in Rome? Always do what the locals do, right?

Even if it is something you'll regret later.

The fact that I was in Vegas gleefully planning to lose forty friggin' dollars was not out of character for me, at all. I was merely using my hall pass from my vacation philosophy. In those days, forty bucks bought two weeks' worth of groceries. And there I was, cheapo me, preparing to throw it away in a matter of hours, if not minutes.

As soon as I dropped my first coin into the slot, I noticed a tingle emerge from somewhere inside my soul. It was the same kind of excitement I felt when I scooped the first spoonful of a hot fudge sundae or opened a box of Whitman's chocolate. The anticipation of what was to come in those circumstances always led me to the point of swooning. All rational thought dissolved into a primitive lust for what was coming next. Gambling was beginning to have the same effect as sugar had on me.

The slot machines I played were Triple 7 machines, the most common machines at the time. I'd gamble a quarter and two white sevens would pop up … not a penny in profit would be paid. I'd lost my money. Mixed colors of triple sevens popped up a few times on the pay line. Twenty quarters! A five-dollar profit, if I didn't count the money I initially gambled. But still …

And then it happened. I put in a single quarter, pulled the lever, stepped over to the next machine to deposit my coin. Before I put it in, I heard the bells go off and saw lights flashing on the machine I stepped away from.

I glanced back at the machine. Three red sevens were lined up. Three red sevens! On the payline! I'd won fifty friggin' dollars! I couldn't believe it!

I was happier than a pig rolling around in rhinestones and mud. I was hooting and hollering when a man from behind said sarcastically, "Too bad you didn't bet TWO quarters."

Why was this stranger raining on my parade? Didn't he see what had just happened? Didn't he ... it was then I happened to look at the top of the machine. I hadn't really paid it heed before, and if I had, I still wouldn't have bet TWO quarters at a time. Who would do such a thing?

But the sinking feeling came over me, one that would stay with me until I arrived back in Minneapolis. If I had only put in one more coin, a measly twenty-five cents, I would have won a thousand dollars.

My initial joy melted into deep regret and feelings of shame. Why was I so cheap? Why did I always have to be so gosh darn thrifty? If I'd only invested another quarter ... and this was also the first time I'd used the term 'invested' connected with gambling ... the winnings would have paid for both our trip and the brake job we put off to head to Vegas.

Downtrodden, I cashed in the rest of my coins and trudged back to the hotel room.

As soon as I opened the door, I started whining to my husband about what I could have won. He interrupted me to begin his lecture on the odds of ever winning in gambling, explaining the basic laws of probability. His sermon ended with the age old "they didn't build Las Vegas on winners, only losers."

That's what I got for marrying someone who minored in mathematics and majored in clichés.

∞

Robert Frost is a favorite poet of mine. As a young teen, I devoured Frost's poetry nightly. Early on, I identified with the hired man in his poem *The Death of the Hired Man*. I sadly understood what Frost meant when he wrote the line "Home is where when you have to go, they have to let you in."

In the verse, the handyman had come 'home' to die which was a bit ironic since he'd hardly been stellar help. He'd usually leave at the time the couple needed him the most. Still, it was one of the few places on earth he felt welcomed over the years. When he needed to find a place to die, it was the only logical choice.

Twenty years and nineteen trips later, I wonder if Las Vegas has become that place for me, a place where they have to let me in. And a place where, if I paid any attention to my doctor's warnings, I could easily die.

11

Issues

Traveling two thousand miles to Las Vegas by a combination of automobile, train, and bus were somewhat hampered by my health issues. There were days when I couldn't make it across my living room without screaming in pain. The myriad of my escalating problems made going anywhere, except the nearest urgent care, a highly questionable adventure.

Physical obstacles are common among the overweight elderly. Yet, I never think of myself in that exact terminology. Rather, I am merely "kind of old" and "kind of obese". The term 'kind of' is one of my favorite qualifiers. It allows me to use the correct term 'old' and 'obese" to describe myself, yet somehow softens the blow.

I've never been one who excels in self-awareness. That singular concept is beyond my limited capabilities. I have no idea how others perceive me, or perhaps choose not to know. Instead, I believe every person I encounter jumps head first into my river of self-denial.

In an era when releasing private medical information is criminal, I have few reservations on divulging mine. Besides, most of them are painfully obvious. You'd never mistake me for a marathon runner. Or a mall walker.

I am one hundred pounds overweight. No tunic top, no matter how "long and flowing" will hide that little fact. I might be able to conceal five or ten pounds, but industrial strength Spandex could not hide what I'd like hidden. And, though I blog about being a large woman, make jokes about it on stage in front of a hundred strangers, I have difficulty typing the exact number of my excess poundage. But, it's not just my weight that I would like to forget about. My health problems are one gigantic snowball growing bigger with each passing day.

My high blood pressure caused my congestive heart failure. CHF caused my heart arrhythmia. Arrhythmia led to a stroke. Having a stroke meant I had to have an MRI. During the MRI, the radiologist discovered a benign brain tumor. The position of my tumor proves that one's grey matter is prime real estate. The only thing that matters is location, location, location. The growth, though small at the moment, is situated directly behind my eye socket. It if grows any larger, it can cause life-threatening seizures and blindness. My one hope is that it continues to grow at a snail's pace.

The other hope I hold dear is that I make it to Las Vegas and home again, alive and in one piece.

∞

Vegas isn't the best place for a person with bad knees either. Bad knees can be caused by an injury, obesity, or jogging for decades on concrete or asphalt surfaces. In my case, I was born with knees that were not normal. Decades of being overweight only added to my unseen birth defect. My kneecaps do not align but sit slightly off center, creating friction and rubbing away at the cartilage as they pull to the side, missing the natural groove that allows knees to function with ease.

I wasn't aware of the issue until my knees started falling apart bit by bit in my forties. One day I stood up and it felt like a knife was being plunged into my left knee. Five hours and one CAT scan later, my doctor was telling me I needed to undergo surgery to relieve the pain and further destruction. Unfortunately, the surgery that was meant to save my knees destroyed them.

Before my kneecaps crumbled, I was a very active fat lady. I loved long distance biking. My maximum one-day ride was eighty miles on a forest bike trail. Any memory of my annual Vegas trips included gleefully walking the three-mile strip over and over, a smile on my contented face. After the lateral release surgery on my knee, any exercise that involved the use of my legs skidded to a halt. The slightest misstep or turn and my knee would reinjure itself, swelling to double its size. The pain would be unbearable. For days, all I could do was lounge on a recliner, an ice bag on each knee. With every passing breath, I vowed to never let a surgeon touch any part of my body, ever again.

I'm grateful my mobility isn't bad enough I am forced to use an electronic scooter to maneuver around Wal-Mart. Yet, in any big box store I hold on tightly to the shopping cart, leaning over the handle for support as I hobble down the aisles. The thought of buying anything from the lower shelves never crosses my mind. I cannot do that simple act. At the check out line, if I drop a penny or a quarter it becomes the property of whoever finds it.

∞

Broken Heart

A decade and a half ago I was diagnosed with congestive heart failure. The walls of my heart thickened as its power to pump blood through my system faltered. The harder my heart worked to accomplish its primary goal, the weaker I became. There wasn't enough oxygen or nutrients streaming through my system to meet my needs. By the time I reluctantly made it to the doctor for an examination, I could barely keep my eyes open.

The doctor immediately ordered an overnight stay in a sleep center. He was convinced my heart failure was caused by sleep apnea, indicating my snoring was a sign. If that were the case, I've had sleep apnea since I was a toddler.

I've endured complaints about my snoring all of my life: from siblings, to roommates, to folks on the other side of a building. Thirty years ago, my husband and I stayed in a fancy lodge up north. At checkout, I recognized the couple in front of me. They'd stayed in the room across the hall. For five minutes they yelled at the clerk about the incredibly loud snoring that traveled across the hall and into their suite. The man hollered about the hotel renting a room to a "damn angry" bear. The woman claimed their honeymoon had been ruined. They didn't sleep a wink, all night long. The clerk refused to refund their money. As they left, they each shot a hateful look at my husband.

My husband doesn't snore. He doesn't make a single sound when he slumbers. I was the damn angry bear who ruined a honeymoon night.

When I left the sleep clinic, I was outfitted with not only a sleep machine, mask and hose, but a handful of prescription medication that I'd have to take for the rest of my life.

A thought crossed my mind that maybe I was getting old.

Fortunately, once again, I dismissed it.

∞

Lucky Stroke

One Friday morning, two and a half years ago, I felt a slight "ping" go off in my head. Instantly, my world turned digital. I was trapped, floating upside down inside a liquid mosaic.

Being me, the extraordinary-dysfunctional-figure-out-every-single-damn-thing on your own me, I made my way to my computer. It didn't cross my mind to call 911. Nor to call my husband, who was on an all day bike ride. As usual, I was alone in facing my demons in life.

It took a half hour for my vision to clear. The chair no longer looked like it was constructed from jigsaw pieces. The door to my office didn't belong on the set of the Twilight Zone. Nothing about it was wobbly or squishy. Clicking the computer on, I Googled my symptoms. If WebMd turned out to be right, I'd just survived a stroke.

I still have my notes from my GP. "Patient suffered a cerebral infarction in the right PCA territory." In layman terms, it was an ischemic stroke that resulted from a blockage in one of my blood vessels. The word infarction means the tissue surrounding the vessel that exploded died.

Died as in dead. Dead-dead. No recovery of the tissue was possible. No hope for rejuvenation of the tissue. A portion of my brain was literally as I claimed many times, *Brain Dead.* But this time it was for real, and not just an excuse of why I couldn't make a luncheon.

Except for sheer exhaustion, a major year-long depression of biblical proportions, a loss of twenty-five percent of my peripheral vision, I actually felt the same as I did before the stroke. I knew I was lucky, still I was baffled.

When I thought of the phrase *stroke victim,* I assumed there would be slurring of words and crippled limps. I asked, "Doctor why isn't my speech impaired? Why is my mobility the same as before?"

She answered, "You were lucky. The vessel that burst was on the right side of the brain. The left side of the brain controls language and movement."

"What does the right side do? Specifically the portion where my brain was damaged? " I asked, dreading to hear her answer, terrified of what I could no longer do.

"Actually," she said, "we don't really know what that part of the brain does. It does something, but we have no idea."

A list of possibilities ran through my brain. Maybe it was the section that could predict the winning power ball numbers. Or maybe it was my direct line to God or Buddha. Or one day I would just stop in mid-stride, turn into salt and never move again.

My GP stopped my exaggerated paranoia to add a dose of frightening truth. "But there is something else," she said. "Nothing to be that worried about right now, but the MRI revealed a benign tumor. It shouldn't be an issue, unless it grows ..."

∞

For one of the few times in my life, my fears were justified. I was terrified traveling to Las Vegas alone. A four-thousand mile round trip where anything could happen from a car accident, a train plummeting off a cliff, or being mugged in Las Vegas.

This time it wasn't an accident on the road that concerned me. Instead it was a car crash inside my body that was waiting to happen.

But I knew one thing. There were so many things wrong with me that there was no reason not to travel. It was painfully obvious I was going to die sooner, than later.

And if somehow I have a choice?

It has to be Las Vegas, the saddest and happiest place on earth.

Preparation

The cliché, planning for a journey is the most rewarding part of travel, is true for me. The excitement of what could, will, or might happen far exceeds anything that actually happens during my adventures. Having a mild case of obsessive-compulsion disorder, I relish in packing, unpacking, packing again, unpacking, and then doing a final repacking. For a long vacation, such as Vegas, I begin preparing three months in advance.

I love making lists, crossing off lists, making new lists and being prepared for anything that might possibly go wrong while traveling. The precise organization that I spend on my rambling is exactly the opposite of how I live my daily life.

Though I tend to make two or three to-do lists a day, I rarely complete any of the chores. The small piece of paper I write on is usually lost by dinnertime. Even posting it on a clever online bulletin board website does not work for me. I've tried slapping a brightly colored Post-it on my wall as a reminder. The Post-it will eventually fall off and slide underneath my desk, hidden by file drawers and kicked-off house slippers.

Five years later I will occasionally find one of my dated manifests. My half-a-decade-old note is the same one I wrote to myself earlier that morning:

1) Clean house
2) Do laundry
4) Exercise
5) Count calories
3) Write two thousand words or at least a friggin' paragraph.

More than likely, none of my goals will be accomplished or even attempted. My house has never been actually clean, at least not according to my mom's standards. Our floors are only mopped when I can no longer pass off the dirt as built-in tile patterns. Laundry is accomplished in steps, often one pantie at a time. My daily writing and word count averages zero to five hundred words max.

Still, making a to-do list is a part of my psyche, like buying a new notebook when I start a project. There is an urge to create that same excitement I felt on the very first day of school.

Every city I travel to has its own separate checklist. The one for Las Vegas includes items for that city, and that city alone:

Sunglasses on a cord
One tube of SPF 30
Animal print, rhinestone and bedazzled clothing
Diaper pins
Temporary tramp stamps

I am at the age where survival is more important than style. Long ago, my stilettos were tossed aside for shoes that could only be described as sturdy. If I need to carry anything like a purse or glasses, I attach it to my body. I acknowledge that my being careless is a given. My ability to forget anything, no matter how important, will happen. If my sunglasses are not lashed securely, I will lose them.

The sun is painfully bright walking down the Vegas strip. For my weakening, stroke injured-eyes, it is not an option to go without shades. The Nevada sun easily turns into a lethal weapon. I do not want to become one of its victims.

The Vdara hotel opened on Las Vegas Boulevard in December of 2009. It took a few months before its one architectural flaw, nicknamed *The Death Ray*, made headline news across the world. The Vdara is a fifty-seven story hotel/condo complex comprised of steel beams and mirrored windows. Though lovely to look at, Vdara came close to having their poolside guests spontaneously combust.

The concave design of the mirrored building acted as a parabolic reflector, collecting the bright Las Vegas sun's burning energy and shooting the beams downward toward the chaise lounges surrounding the pool. The laser like beams were so intense they could easily burn skin at certain times of the day because of the sun's unique positioning. When the sunrays were aimed just so, plastic cups and bags melted in the heat. Vdara eventually fixed the issue by using strategically placed gigantic green plants around the pool area and installing light filtering film on the window surfaces. Still the image of being spiked to death by a sunray bounding off a glass building has stayed with many people. It has with me.

In Vegas, if I am not inside a casino, I am usually strolling by one. If not, I'll be lounging on a chaise next to the pool. I always wear SPF 30 sunscreen. Once it is applied, my entire body shines as bright as the fake bling on my chubby fingers.

If I am not careful in rubbing the sunscreen completely into my skin before I bolt from the hotel room, it will be noticeable when I hit the casino floor. There are many times in the past when I've looked like a mime in training as I walked the strip. If I added a pair of white gloves, I could have earned a few bucks as a street entertainer.

Leopard is the new black

When I am in Sin City, leopard is the new black. Minnesota winters mean my daily outfit consists of a pair of black sweatpants topped off with a black hoodie. If I'm feeling festive, I might toss on a gray sweatshirt featuring a tiny, embroidered loon sitting atop my left breast. My summer ensembles are no better or more colorful. I don dark t-shirts and black, stretch capris. I slip my feet into scruffy, Velcro strapped white New Balance shoes. If my clothes make any statement, it's "Don't look at me. Please, I beg you."

But in Vegas … it's a whole different story. Everyone, including me, wants to be noticed.

When you visit Vegas the one thing you will continually notice is skin … rippling and jiggling mountains of it coming at you in varying hues, ages and genders. Young women squeeze into body tight dresses with hems that are so high and tops so low, there is barely any material left to cover their lady bits. If the outfit happens to be a two-piece, more than likely the skirt will be a low riding hip hugger, and a red lace thong will be riding up her butt crack. On their feet will be sky-high high heels of at least four inches.

I have even seen six-inch heels, the wearer struggling to take one slow step at a time. The fact that the owner held an ice-filled cocktail glass at two in the afternoon probably didn't help her stability. Every forward movement became a true act of bravery. If she toppled over just once, there'd be little chance for survival.

For a long time, the city of Las Vegas itself was the epitome of phoniness. Now the average tourist is counterfeit, as well. From fake nails, eyelashes, hair, tans, tattoos, and jewelry to multiple layers of foam padding that enhance both boobs and butts to Kardashian-sized portions. Nothing in Vegas appears to be real.

Men get trapped in the same game of illusions. They layer spray-on tans and hang gold-plated chains around their necks. Cheap toupees glisten on their heads as they stuff fake money behind one single legit twenty-dollar bill in their wallets. With their wallets wide open, they hold it for a few seconds in that position, allowing those around them to see just how "rich" they are.

The younger men have steroid enhanced bodies that reveal chiseled ribs and six-pack abs that not even

God could create. I have seen men walking down the strip wearing, what had to be a five-inch thick codpiece placed under their jeans in order to attract attention to their Netherlands.

There is nothing wrong with any of the above attitudes when in Vegasland. In fact, it's perfectly acceptable. The city is an adult theme park meant for fantasy, not reality. Simply put, being in Las Vegas means it's Halloween all year long.

From shoes, leggings, tops, swimming suits, underwear and jewelry, my Las Vegas attire is nothing less than a polyester rainforest of animal prints, rhinestones, and sequined anything. I spend a year picking out my Vegas duds. If it's a cheetah print it goes into my shopping cart. If it's on clearance, I often buy two. For a ten-day stay, I will carry enough clothing for three wardrobe changes a day. All of the clothing will still have their sales tags attached when I arrive. They often have the same tags when I leave. If one of the outfits becomes my "lucky" outfit, the one I was wearing when I hit a jackpot, I will wear it the entire trip, rinsing it out nightly in the hotel sink.

Growing up a "hefty" girl who could only find dark colored A-line dresses hidden at the back of the local Sears store, I love the attitude of today's plus-size model and retailer. *Show It if You Got It* is the norm. Gone are the terms such as sensible, sturdy, and concealing. Now the ad copy reads voluptuous, full-figured, big and beautiful. When you add the sparkle and glitter of the clothes I buy for Vegas, I end up looking like a Plus-Size Dolly Parton Drag Queen.

Life doesn't get better than that.

Diaper pins for security.

A reoccurring nightmare I endure finds me completely lost and stranded in Las Vegas. In it, I am filled with dread as I trudge from one semi-familiar gambling hall to the next. I keep asking gamblers or tourists if anyone knows who I am? Not a single person hears what I am asking. I pass by a mirrored wall and catch a glimpse of the reflection of a woman. I have no idea who she is. It is not until I am about to come to consciousness, that I realize she is me.

I wake up terrified, my eyes shooting open. It takes a second or two to know I am in my bed at home, safe and warm beneath a down comforter. My night terrors disappear and I fall back to sleep. Yet, in the morning, I will check my cache of diaper pins in my jewelry box. If I don't have a dozen or more, I will make another online order to purchase them. I would never consider traveling without them.

I don't need a dream interpreter to explain my nightmare. I am petrified of losing three things in Las Vegas: my ID, my return ticket home, and my credit cards.

Because of my severe sleep apnea, I need to book a roomette on Amtrak. Without a machine plugged in, and a mask covering my face, I wake up fifty-eight times an hour. That is not a typo. By the time my condition was diagnosed, I couldn't drive more than twenty minutes before dozing off at the wheel.

A room on Amtrak can be extraordinarily expensive or in my case, free. For the last decade or so I have used frequent rider miles to travel on Amtrak. Throughout the year we charge everything from sofas to a Sunday newspaper in order to earn the forty thousand miles needed for a round trip fare, room and meals included. It is the only first class travel I have ever done. I feel like a big shot the moment I step on the train.

However, if I were to lose my Amtrak ticket while in Vegas? I am screwed, unless I purchased the e-ticket, which is not allowed when using reward miles for travel. Rail tickets are treated like cash. If I lost mine, I'd have to buy another one to replace it.

Unless I win a progressive jackpot, there'd be no way I could justify spending the money that Amtrak demands for first class travel on the spur of the moment. I've long since decided if my tickets did get misplaced, I'd probably decide to stay and live in Vegas. It would be cheaper.

I do everything I can to prevent losing ID's, credit cards, cash or my ticket ... everything including looking foolish.

On every trip I carry a red zippered nylon bag, measuring six by eleven inches. Inside the pouch are two zippered compartments. In the back compartment I place my return ticket and passport. Homeland Security requires both air and rail passengers to carry IDs. If I do not have one, I will not be able to board the train, even with a ticket in hand.

Two diaper pins secure the zipper shut. I do not remove them until the very last evening when I am sitting at McCarran Airport, waiting to catch the Amtrak Shuttle.

In the other compartment is my start-out cash for the trip, six hundred dollars. If I run out of cash after a day or two, I will withdraw three hundred dollars daily from an ATM.

Finally, the pouch goes deep inside my bra and is diaper pinned securely in place. Four pins are clasped together so in case one opens unexpectedly, the other three would prevent the contents from spilling out onto the ground.

It's a good thing that Amtrak doesn't have a metal detector like the airport does. If it did, my boobs would set off alarms.

Temporary Tramp Stamps

Nowadays, when I go anywhere for more than twenty-four hours, I plaster my body with temporary tramp stamps. I do not add tattoos to look cool or pretend I am a motorcycle momma. I do not have a silver nose ring in my nostril nor do I die my hair purple, green and gothic black. There is not a single piercing below my ear lobes. I am not trying to complete any "look."

I am merely trying to save my life.

The majority of women my age do not have tattoos, even the temporary press-on kind that washes away with soap and rubbing alcohol. A few of my peers have indulged in a bit of the ink, but to my knowledge none of my lifelong friends have ever been tatted. Teenage girls did not do that in the '60s, or at least not the ones I hung around. My fundamentalist Christian friends didn't drink beer, go to movies, or dance. And it goes without saying, not one of them would dare let a man near them with anything that was designed to poke.

Tattoos were the territory of our male counterpoints. My brothers returned from the military with honorary discharge papers and one or more images protruding from their biceps. It was a rite of passage for drunk, young men, a million miles away from home.

I envied my brother's tattoos. I remember one bro's blue inked skeleton, a top hat sitting jauntily on the skull's head as a cigarette dangled from its mouth. In 1962, tattoos were almost evil and certainly titillating. I blushed when a neighbor flexed his biceps and the hula girl danced, her hips swaying in his sweat. Years later, once his muscles disappeared and his stomach grew outwards, he said he wished he had tattooed her on his belly, instead.

As a young woman in the '60s, I was expected to spend my hours daydreaming of the perfect husband while learning to use Aqua Net to perfection. Girls were not supposed to consider for a moment to attempt doing what the boys did, and especially not what the men did.

There were other reasons I never considered getting a tattoo. One, I am scared of needles or pain of any kind. The second is I've never made it to my goal weight. What would happen to the butterfly tattoo I longed for when I finally lost weight? Would the artistic image shrivel into a wrinkled, old moth? In almost every area of my life, anything of beauty was put on hold until I reached that magical day of perfection.

Perfection never happened. But medication did, lots of it. And, because of them, I have no choice but to slap on a few tattoos.

Currently, I am on six different pills a day. I swallow one batch in the morning and the next round at 6:30 p.m. exactly. A few of the pills are the difference between life and death according to my doctor. To make matters worse, the medications need to be taken at precisely the same time, every single day.

At home, I have no problem being on time with my meds. Two separate alarm clocks are set to remind me, as well as an iPad alert. But when traveling, I often forget to take my pills. If I do remember my pills, it is way beyond the scheduled time. If it is three hours past my scheduled time, according to my doctor's instructions, I have to skip the pills and wait for the next cycle to begin, all the while crossing my fingers I don't die.

Traveling in my case always means roaming about in a casino where it's impossible to hear an alarm or cellphone. And because this trip meant being alone without a husband or a friend to remind me, I had to find someway to remember to take my meds.

Then it hit me.

Tattoos! One on the front of each of my hands! My hands are always in view while gambling. Or if I'm not at the slots, I'm scooping out goodies from the buffet onto a plate. Both diversions kept my hands directly in my line of sight.

I wasn't willing to get permanent ink, but I'd heard of temporary tattoos, which I knew nothing about. I didn't know how long they'd last, or if they'd start peeling off in the desert heat. I certainly didn't want ink dribbling onto the sidewalk as I strolled the strip.

So, I headed to the place I learn everything these days, YouTube. I entered the words 'temporary tattoo' in the search bar. Thirty-eight thousand nine hundred videos were available. I doubted if there were any videos uploaded by seniors who wanted tramp stamps to remind them to take their Warfarin. I quickly skipped over the videos with the DIY instructions of drawing your own image. I have zero artistic skill.

I placed my cursor over the search bar again, and entered Claire's temporary tattoos. Over twenty-eight hundred results were listed, uploaded by girls nine years of age and up.

I clicked on one featuring two adorable young girls who each, not so carefully applied six tattoos to their faces, and eight more on their arms. I chuckled at their kiddish attitude, not realizing I'd end up doing basically the same thing. Why waste a perfect good temporary tattoo by letting it linger in the bag?

They instructed me to remove the sheet of tattoos from the package and cut around each tattoo. The next step would be pressing a wet cloth on top of the tattoo for ten seconds. The moisture from the cloth would activate the glue and ink in the image and stick the image to my skin. Then I merely peeled off the paper. According to one of the girls, I was to do the same thing over and over until I ran out of tattoos. The other girl explained the tattoos would last for days or until your mom made you wash them off.

The process seemed easy enough. Two weeks before I left for Vegas, I headed for the mall and purchased two packages of tats. One package included colorful stars, hearts, moons, and feathers, plus a few peacocks or two. The second package had no color at all except black. Skulls, crossbones and pirates. When I got home, I slipped them into the bag, planning to open them once I was on the road.

If I did it before hand, I'd probably never stop putting them on, just like the nine-year-old girls on YouTube. I am that much of a kid at heart.

Getting There

Minneapolis St. Paul International Airport is a ten-minute drive from our home. From there, a flight to Las Vegas is roughly three hours and twenty minutes. Any day of the week, I can be in Las Vegas in less time than it takes to watch a Martin Scorsese movie. Instead, in order to reach my gambling mecca, I travel two thousand plus miles by a combination of car, train, and shuttle bus.

Taking Valium, drinking tequila, or undergoing hypnosis never helped ease my fear of flying. Marrying an air traffic controller didn't help either. It wasn't that Steve brought home tales of terror during his twenty-seven years at Minneapolis St. Paul International Airport. He didn't. During his tenure at MSP, nothing dangerous happened under his watch. Nothing. Nada. Not a single incident could justify my position that if God really wanted us to fly in a machine capable of spiraling downward at four hundred miles an hour, he'd have made the earth a bouncy castle.

In fact, the safety record at MSP multiplied my anxieties. It bolstered my 'if not now, when?' OCD thought process. My fear of flying—or rather my angst at sitting in a cushioned seat thirty-three thousand feet off the ground—was mine alone.

From early childhood, I'd wallowed in every air disaster I heard on the evening news. My brother worked at Chicago's Midway Airport. If a crash happened, I'd wait anxiously for him to return at night. He'd tell me horror stories of body parts strewn across the tarmac. I'd scream and put my head under my blanket. Whether these memories are true or not are up for discussion. I was a writer and fantasizer before I came to the age of reason and reality.

However, it's not the actual flying part that bothers me. It's the height that an airplane can reach. Fear of falling off of anything higher than a barstool is terrifying to me.

Decades ago, my husband and I traveled to Chicago for a weekend of fun. I searched for a hotel near Michigan Avenue. I chose one that boasted of its atrium design and massive indoor foliage. It was the dead of winter, and anything green sounded good to me. I didn't bother to research what a hotel atrium might look like. I figured it was an open space with lots of plants and light. What could be wrong with that?

As we walked into the lobby, my heart clinched. The atrium ceiling was twenty-five stories high and every single room was visible from where I stood. The landings encircled the atrium, floor after floor, with only a chest high glass railing on each landing to protect guests from tumbling to their deaths. Plus, the only way up or down included a ride in a glass elevator.

Second floor, I thought to myself, *I can handle second floor. Maybe the third. But, no higher, definitely not.*

My husband gave the receptionist our names as I stood there plotting a getaway if lower rooms were not available. I thought of announcing that I planned on filing for divorce immediately. My unexpected proclamation would let me walk out of the hell I found myself in, my head held high in perceived self-justification. That little lie of marital disharmony seemed way more appealing than taking a ride in a glass elevator.

I watched as one of four elevators travelled the atrium's twenty-five floors. It amazed me that not a single passenger treated it with the respect that a Wes Craven amusement park ride for the acrophobic deserved. Not a single occupant was pounding on the door in terror as the lift moved silently up or down.

Standing behind my husband I leaned in close and whispered, "Ask for a lower floor."

He said to the clerk, "Do you have any rooms high up?"

Steve doesn't support my phobias. Nor does he pay them any attention, whatsoever.

"We have a room on the twenty-third floor," she responded.

"Great," Steve said, right before I kicked his foot.

I briefly wondered if I could get both our cats in the divorce settlement.

My husband walked quickly to the elevator as I trudged slowly behind, trying to decide if I could get him to walk up the emergency stairs to our room. In the old days before we had sex, I could get him to do anything. Now I have to buy him a Lamborghini to get him to mow the lawn.

Apparently, my anxiety was evident on my face. With a hint of disdain he asked, "Don't tell me you're afraid of the elevators too?"

Generally, my answer would be no. I am not afraid of elevators, at all. They're a piece of cake, unless they are made with glass and I can actually see what is happening. It's easy to forget you are one hundred feet above ground when you're enclosed in a steel box.

I didn't bother to answer.

We stepped into the small, crowded space. A loud, bored - with - his - wife's - phobias sigh escaped from his clutched throat. I closed my eyes and didn't dare open them. I could feel the elevator move upward, stopping every few seconds to let someone on or off. Finally, the door opened and I heard my husband say, "Let's go."

Miraculously, we'd arrived safely at the twenty-third floor. I made my way out of the elevator, my eyelids squeezed tight. When I knew I was planted safely in the hallway, I opened them, expecting a wave of relief to comfort me. Instead, a panic attack took hold of me, the likes of which I'd never experienced.

A few feet ahead of me was the glass railing that ran along the atrium side of the hallway. It easily came to the top of my chest, yet I could envision myself tumbling over it and rapidly crashing into the marble tile, twenty-three floors below. My body would splatter like red pellets from a paint gun.

Realistically of course, that wouldn't happen. Not unless someone hoisted me over the railing. I quickly calculated my husband's strength potential. Nah, he couldn't lift me even if he wanted to … a scenario growing more likely by each passing minute. But someone else could lift me. Some unknown bodybuilding hit man lurking nearby who …

Or perhaps I would defy the law of physics and accidentally fall over the railing all by myself.

Even if I didn't fall, being that high up still scared the bejeebees out of me. Once again, I squeezed my eyes shut and tried to figure out a way to get to my room. I placed my palms firmly against the wall behind me. I edged my way, step-by-step, inch-by-inch, as I slid my outstretched hands along the wall. I looked like Spiderman's obese mom out for her daily constitutional.

When we finally made it to our suite, I stepped inside knowing I would not be going out of the room until we checked out on Monday morning. I had just blown hundreds of dollars on a fun-filled mini vacation, only to spend the entire time in a hotel room, alone. I didn't expect Steve to stay inside the room with me. It wasn't fair. It was his vacation, too.

After a few minutes of his balking and lecturing me on the stupidity of my fears, I pointed out that just because I was a prisoner in the hotel didn't mean he would have to be one. He was free to do whatever he wanted to do in Chicago, but he had to do it on his own. He could go to the action movies he'd like to see, eat at the health food restaurants he'd never enter if I was anywhere within his radar, shop at stores where nothing was on clearance. The city was his for the taking.

His eyes lit up the moment he 'got it'. He could act like he would act if he were single once again. To this day, as far as my husband is concerned, the weekend I spent trapped inside a twenty-third floor room, is one of the best vacations of our married life.

∞

Catching the Train

Amtrak's Empire Builder, originates in Seattle, and arrives daily at the St. Paul Amtrak station, a thirty-minute drive from where I live. The train continues East to Chicago where it arrives an hour too late to catch the connecting Southwest Chief, heading to Los Angeles. Consequently, if I chose to ride Amtrak from my hometown, I'd have to spend a night in downtown Chicago, adding to the cost of my trip, both ways. Instead, I drive three hundred and eighty-six miles to Fort Madison, Iowa where I board the Southwest Chief on the same day I leave home.

Driving from Minneapolis to Fort Madison, Iowa is a no brainer for me. It's a pleasant seven-hour drive through Iowa farmland and includes the possibility of two casino stops along the way. A gambler's road trip doesn't get any better than that, unless you add a buffet, which I always do.

With a recent stroke hovering in my background, and the possibility of another one clouding my future, making the trip alone was a bit more worrisome than usual. This time, I asked my husband if he'd like to go at least part of the way with me. I sweetened the deal by suggesting he bring his bike and ride with me to Northwoods, Iowa where we could spend the night at Diamond Jo's Casino and Resort. The next morning he could cycle the one hundred and seventeen miles home.

Yes, we are that different.

Steve agreed and I was thrilled. One less day alone on the road sounded good to me.

∞

It was two in the afternoon when we checked into the hotel at Diamond Jo's. The lobby sparkled with cleanliness. The smell of freshly baked chocolate chip cookies drifted over from the free coffee bar. From the registration desk, we could see through glass doors to the hallway that led to the hotel rooms and the large indoor pool. No one was swimming. No one ever swims at a casino hotel pool. The average guest wasn't there to stay healthy.

My husband and I headed up to our second floor room. The wife in me won over my urge to ask him to carry the luggage to the room while I dashed to the casino. Instead, I trotted along, pretending I had little interest in discarding him to begin my gambling.

The double room with two queen-sized beds was large and spacious and featured a large, flat screen TV, microwave and refrigerator. A free USA today newspaper was provided as well. I feigned interest in reading for a few minutes. Nothing caught my interest. Nor could it. A few hundred yards away bells were ringing and jackpots were being won.

I fluffed the pillows and propped them up on the bed. I leaned back, opened my laptop and clicked on the internet. I checked out the Amtrak website to see if that day's Southwest Chief was running on time. It was, and I made the assumption the next day's train would be on time as well.

Steve walked to the window and looked out across the parking lot. He said, "Hey, I think the history center is open across the street. You want to go?"

"Not really. Do you mind if I stay here and wait for you?"

I am not a good liar.

He responded, "Yeah, right. I'll find you in the casino when I'm ready for dinner."

"Well, if I'm not in the room, when you get back then maybe I ..."

He didn't bother to acknowledge my cover-up but grabbed his jacket and headed out of the room.

I gave him five minutes to reach the elevator and leave the building before I bolted toward the door. It was good to be alone to do what I wanted to do, and to do it by myself.

I could never be married to anyone who expected me to spend every single moment with him. Nor would any man or woman want to spend every single moment of his day with me. Of that I am sure.

I refer to us as married yet monogamous singles. When we are on vacations, we have breakfast together then go our separate ways, meeting again for dinner and later, a show. We live our day-to-day life exactly the same way.

For a gambling woman married to a non-gambling man, this is the perfect arrangement. I would hate it if he wanted to tag along with me to the slots. Or if he insisted on sitting next to me as I pressed the same button a thousand times over. I've seen husbands who sit quietly holding their wife's purse, hour after hour. I'd give up gambling before I'd do that to my husband.

Three hours later and fifty-eight dollars richer, I was sitting at a Walking Dead slot machine when my husband walked up to me.

"How you doing?" he asked.

"Good," I answered. "I won enough to pay for the buffet."

Already I was a winner and Vegas still lay ahead.

∞

By 7:00 a.m. the next morning, my husband was standing outside the hotel preparing for his ride back home. I stood at our hotel room window and managed to catch his eye and waved a hearty goodbye. As soon as he pedaled off into the sunrise, I rushed to open my makeup bag.

Inside were the two packages of temporary tattoos I'd purchased. I used my manicure scissors to carefully cut around them. I planned on using two at a time, one for each hand. I brought the extra, just in case one fell off. I grabbed a wet washcloth and sat down to experiment.

I chose a colorful blue and green peacock design for my right hand. I placed the design on the top of my hand and pressed down with the wet washcloth. I counted to thirty Mississippi and removed the cloth. I carefully peeled back the paper. The image was actually quite lovely. My hand turned from an old lady's claw to an art exhibition. I choose a heart for the top of my left hand.

And then, well, I couldn't stop. The skin up and down my arms suddenly seemed barren and wanting of decoration. What the heck? My conservative husband was nowhere to be seen. I was alone. And it was pre-Vegas, right?

I added another tattoo, then another and before I knew it twenty minutes had passed. I had eighteen tattoos plastered across my body: on my forearms, thighs, tits and stomach. I had to resist, unlike the two nine-year-old girls on YouTube who chose not to resist, placing a few on my cheeks.

I looked down. My bag of tats was nearly empty. By the time I left the hotel to continue my drive to Fort Madison, I looked like a sixty-six-year-old carney worker. I've never been more pleased.

Iowa to New Mexico

The five-hour drive from the Minnesota border to Fort Madison, Iowa included learning the fine art of applying manure. I love talk radio when I am on the road, not the kind featuring raging pundits, but local call-in stations where folks rant about traffic in a town with a population of two hundred or rattled on for hours about the problems with begonias. Nowadays, the most popular shows are radio yard sales where callers announce personal items for sale on the air.

The radio host asked, "Caller Seven, what do you have to sell today?"

An elderly lady responded, "I have a pair of white Venetian blinds, fifty-four inches long. There's a dent or two but they work. I'd like five dollars for the pair."

"And your phone number is …."

And Caller Seven *actually* responded with their phone number for *everyone* in the county to hear. The city girl in me reeled at their naiveté. The mystery author in me began plotting … "*A psycho listens to the radio station. He hears the venetian blind pitch. He thinks if he had those venetian blinds he could kill someone with the cord. He wants those Venetian blinds no matter what. Maybe he'll even kill stupid Caller Seven for being so naïve. Maybe he'd even use the venetian blinds to do so ...*"

Fortunately, another item a caller was selling caught my attention. I forgot about my extraordinarily amateur plot featuring a psycho who wanted window decoration to do his dirty work.

After hours of listening to one station after another, I turned off of Highway 218 South onto a shortcut I discovered a few years ago. On a two-lane country road, I meandered past sprawling farms, garage sales, churches, and hopeful B&Bs located in the middle of nowhere.

When I reached the Mississippi River town of Fort Madison, I pulled into the parking lot at the city's library. I raced inside and used their Internet access to check my email. Once on board the Southwest Chief, I would not have access to the Web for thirty-six hours or more. As soon as I was finished, I rushed to the station.

The Amtrak station is located at the Burlington Northern Santa Fe freight yard. The connecting buildings belonged to the BNSF railroad, along with the majority of the parking lot spaces. I arrived at least an hour early to secure a parking spot, whose availability varied depending upon the amount of workers on the freight line on any given day. Parking is free for Amtrak riders and a safe place to leave a car for weeks on-end. Railway bulls, age-old slang for a railroad's company security guards, roam the property twenty-four seven.

I pulled into the lot and squeezed into a narrow spot, wedged between two dented pickups. Reaching into my purse, I removed a twenty-dollar bill and placed it along with a spare car key into the glove box. If I end up leaving Vegas penniless, or manage to lose my car key, though it will be safely pinned to the inside of my purse, I'll be able to get back home.

I stepped out of the car and popped open my trunk, grabbed the small duffle bag and hung it over my shoulder. I lifted out my wheeled luggage. Clicking the key fob, I heard a double *beep-beep*, assuring me the car was completely locked. I checked the doors just to make sure. Eventually, after only four repeats of the same beeping and checking, my OCD retreated into the background and I could walk away. I headed past dozens of cars to reach the red brick building.

"Good evening," I said to the railroad attendant behind the counter. I handed her my ticket and driver's license. I knew the drill. "Is the train running on time?"

"It's twelve minutes late," she answered.

I knew that figure could change at any time, making the train even later. "Is it full?"

"Always," she said. "It's spring break and then there are the Amish heading to Tijuana, Mexico, for medical treatment."

The Amish community rejects medical insurance as being part of the secular world. The elders of the church have managed to secure bottom line medical prices in Mexico for their fellow believers, assuring the Mexican providers that their fellow Amish brethren not only paid in cash, but rarely sued for malpractice. After all, the outcome is totally in God's hands. And what sense does it make to sue God?

The train station's waiting room had three rows of eight chairs, a water fountain, and a pay phone. Old magazines were scattered on a low table, along with a few coloring books for kids. Amtrak route guides and brochures filled a metal rack. The room's large windows looked out over railroad tracks that ran parallel to the Mississippi River.

Ten minutes later an Amish family consisting of a young man and woman and two small children arrived. Shortly later, another set of Amish men shuffled in.

One by one, three older non-Amish women showed up, pulling their luggage behind them. The Amish sat isolated in the corner. The three women and I chatted about our destinations.

"Where are you heading?" I asked the woman wearing a matching pink hoodie and sweat pants.

"To see the grandkids in St Louis. And you?"

"I'm getting off at Los Angeles but continuing on to Las Vegas," I informed the trio.

No one asked me why I was making such an arduous trip by train. Each of us probably rode the train for the same good reason. It stayed firmly planted on

God's good earth, unless of course, it tumbled off the side of a mountain.

"How long does that take you?" the eighty-some year old asked. She stood bundled up in her grey winter coat.

"Forty-four hours," I answered. "Thirty-six hours to L.A. Then Vegas is another seven-hour shuttle ride. But …," I hesitated to get into it, but I plowed ahead anyway, "I do have a car rental reservation in case I decide to drive from L.A. to Vegas, instead of riding on the shuttle. It's quicker."

Way quicker. I've driven the two hundred sixty miles from Union Station to Las Vegas in four hours. But, this time, I had no idea if I'd have the energy to make the drive. I didn't know how I would feel physically, once I made it to Los Angeles. I'd wait and see before I made any decision.

Each of us continually checked our watches. The train was now thirty-three minutes late. Finally, the attendant's voice boomed over the intercom, "The Southwest Chief will be arriving in six minutes. Please bring your luggage and meet me outside the building. I will show you where to stand on the platform."

The railroad attendant pointed me in the direction of the far west end of the platform while directing the others in the opposite direction. The coach seats were at the rear of the train, the first class cars at the front. The observation car and the dining car separated the two types of travelers.

I'm a slow walker, so the train arrived before I reached my "stand here" mark. My sleeping car attendant was aware ahead of time that I was getting on board. From inside, he placed a metal step outside the doorway and then stepped outside. He waved at me from the distance.

"You must be Miss Dennis," he remarked as I finally reached him. He took my two pieces of luggage and hoisted them on the train.

"Yep," I nodded, and with his help, climbed on board.

"I've made a dinner reservation," my car attendant announced as he took hold of my wheeled luggage and slid it into the storage area. "You can go to the dining car as soon as you'd like."

A reservation is required in the dining car for both lunch and dinner. Seating is done in fifteen-minute increments, the last taking place at 8:00 p.m.

"Thanks, Tom," I answered, taking the time to read his nametag. "Can you make my bed as soon as I go to dinner?"

"No problem." He pointed at my duffle bag. "You need help with that going up the stairs?"

"Nah," I answered. "One more thing, I'd like my bed down the entire way."

"All righty," he answered without a hint of surprise.

A lot of passengers prefer to travel like I do, with the bed opened for their entire trip. My legs are stretched out in front of me. My junk is piled all around. I lean back on fluffed pillows. I am so comfortable in my room on Amtrak that at home, when battling insomnia, I visualize an Amtrak roomette, warm and cozy as the movement of the train rocks me to sleep.

I gingerly climbed up the metal stairs to the upper level as my duffle bag slammed into the stairwell walls. My roomette sat midway down the corridor. I opened the door and placed the luggage on one of the two seats. A total of ten roomettes are on the upper level. We share one toilet. The five bedroom compartments on the same level each have a toilet in their room. On the lower level are four additional roomettes, a shower room, two more toilets for general use, a family bedroom that sleeps up to four, and a handicapped accessible bedroom with its own toilet.

According to the Amtrak website, a roomette is three feet wide by six feet six inches long. On each end is a high back, fabric seat which folds down into a bed. The upper berth is locked into place, allowing for headroom when sitting. The berth remains in that position until it is unlocked and lowered by the attendant, allowing a passenger to climb up into it to sleep.

For me the lower bed, comprised of the two chairs unfolded, is extremely comfortable. I've shared a roomette twice, once with my husband and one time with a female friend. Both times my fellow riders hated sleeping in the roomette.

The upper berth is two feet wide, six foot two inches long. The headroom is extremely limited. My husband is six feet tall and broad shouldered. To him, lying on the bed felt like a coffin. Surprisingly, my much shorter friend despised it as well. A frequent rider on European trains, she was surprised at how uncomfortable and scary Amtrak berths were. In Europe, the stepladders are built into the design of the berth, making the climb far easier. The ladder was also something one could hold onto for support in mid-air. The fact that she had to hoist herself up, while standing only on an armrest, wasn't the only issue with the sleeping arrangement. Once she was on top, she couldn't turn over unless she used her hand to turn her body. Because she tosses and turns in her sleep, she was constantly being jolted awake all night by her forced movements.

The other thing that flabbergasted her was the lack of a guardrail. Only a few straps hung from the ceiling and hooked into the bed frame, supposedly providing protection from tumbling out of bed and crashing onto the floor five feet below. Like my friend said, it is a balancing act to get your ass into bed, much less stay there.

Fortunately, for this trip, I had the room all to myself. I didn't have to worry about seeing a body tumble down from above when I slept.

I rummaged through my luggage a bit and headed to the dining car, two sleeper cars behind me. As I walked the narrow aisle, the movement of the train shifted me from side to side. I used my hands on the walls to steady myself and prevent falling head first on to the carpet. The rail line is notoriously bumpy once the train crosses into Missouri. It doesn't settle down again until Western Kansas.

The train had a total of three sleeper cars, including the one for employees. As I passed through each car, I pressed a button that opened the next door. Eventually I stood at the entrance to the dining car, waiting to be noticed by the dining car attendant.

When dining on Amtrak, you're assigned a seat at a particular table. Dining is served community style. Who, or how many, you end up sitting with at a table is the luck of the draw. A single table sits up to four people.

Talkative riders filled the car. The attendant gestured to the booth on his right. Three people were already seated at the table. I breathed a sigh of relief. I was given the outside seat, directly on the aisle.

As a big, and sometimes bigger woman, fitting into an Amtrak booth can be an issue. When I weighed an astonishing forty more pounds, my belly not only reached over the table as I squeezed painfully into the booth, but it took the tablecloth with it upon my departure. For the rest of that trip I ate alone in my roomette. Having meals delivered by the car attendant is an option for first class passengers. However, it is not something I prefer to do. I enjoyed the company of strangers more than myself.

I slid into the bench seat and said, "Hi, I'm Pat."

The others followed suit with their own introductions. Community dining serves up conversation as well as food.

"I'm Harold, this is Edith," said the man seated across from me. His wife sat demurely besides him.

"I'm Tim," the large man on my right added. If either Tim or I weighed just one pound more each, we'd never be able to sit next to each other. If he were left-handed, we'd be fighting for elbow space just to cut our meat.

The car attendant held out a menu to me. He asked, "Would you care for something to drink first?"

Amtrak serves a variety of cocktails, beer and wines. However, the cost of an alcoholic beverage is not included in the first class package.

"Just water," I answered, suggesting with a wave of my hand that I didn't need the menu. "I already know what I'm ordering."

I'd memorized the calorie count of every item on the menu. Online, Amtrak posted the Southwest Chief menu and nutrition information. I aimed to keep my calories under 1,700 for the day. With a bit of luck, considering all the walking I'd do once I hit Vegas, plus the hours of finger aerobics at the slots, I might lose a pound or two by the end of the trip.

"I'll have the Signature steak, medium well. And just the veggies please, no potato," I instructed. The steak dinner served with a baked potato topped with sour cream, and a mixed medley of veggies was posted online at 945 calories. I easily knocked off 250 calories by avoiding the loaded spud. I didn't bother to include the calories for the small iceberg lettuce house salad, with its few shreds of carrot and slices of tomato. I'd eat around the crotons on top of it and not add the packaged Paul Newman salad dressing provided.

The other passengers at the table were already enjoying their meals. The man and his wife were having the vegetarian plate (455 calories). The man seated next to me was devouring the half-roasted chicken with a side of rice (1370 calories).

Harold and Edith retired eight years earlier, but it was only this year they were about to travel. They waited until "Audrey Hepburn" their pet Pomeranian, passed. Audrey lived to be fifteen years old. Edith reached into her wallet and pulled out a tiny, pink rhinestone decorated framed picture of the dog.

Gorgeous.

"I can see why you named her after a movie star. She's beautiful," I said, not wanting to acknowledge the pain I was feeling at the moment. It had only been a year since I'd lost not only the best cat in the world, but my best friend, Lila.

"Are you on vacation?" I asked Joe.

"Nah, heading to a conference in Flagstaff. Work related."

"What do you do?" I asked.

"Geophysicist," he replied.

"And that is?" I asked, feigning ignorance.

He gave the answer meant for simpletons. "I study earthquakes."

I asked, "Any chance the big one in L.A. is going to happen within the next thirty-five hours? I'm getting off the train in L.A. before heading to Vegas."

"I'd be more worried about Vegas than L.A." he replied.

My eyes widen. "An earthquake?"

He answered, "Nah, the gambling."

And so the conversation went for the hour or so. The three of us talked about pets, natural disasters, and the possibility of California falling into the ocean before I hit a jackpot. I inquired about every single disaster movie I could think of that featured an earthquake, wondering how realistic they were. Joe assured me none of them were.

After turning down the free dessert offered, I headed back to my room. On the way I stopped in the loo. Something was different for me on this trip. Every half hour I wanted to pee. Every thirty friggin' minutes! The constant jiggling movement of the train put my bladder into relief mode. If it continued, I wondered if I'd sleep though the night. For the first time ever I wished I had a bedroom compartment.

There is a major advantage to riding in the much cheaper roomette. The beds run parallel with the tracks. In a one-bedroom compartment, the beds are positioned horizontally across the tracks. When the train stops or lurches, when lying down, your body will naturally roll forward or backward. A friend, who rode in a one-bedroom cross-country said she was constantly stopping herself from falling out of bed. She didn't sleep a wink all night, terrified she'd roll off and break a hip when she hit the floor.

I've never felt that way in the roomette. I've never felt anything but safe.

Once I reached my room, I saw that my SCA (sleeper car attendant) had turned down my bed. He'd set out both pillows for me, and pulled the blanket from the top berth. I slipped off my shoes and positioned myself on the bed. I pulled the curtains that hung over both the door and the hall windows closed. The Velcro didn't quite line up, but I'd learn to expect that. I traveled enough on Amtrak to carry a few extra diaper pins to clamp the curtains together. Finally, when I could no longer see into the hallway, I assumed no one could see into my room.

I focused on the windows looking out at the darkening horizon. Scenes of Missouri passed by with its rolling hills and partially snow covered land. On my return trip, green would be the dominant color of the landscape, as the last of the snow and brown and yellow foliage naturally disappeared.

I clicked on my cell phone and texted my husband I was on the train. I also texted a few friends who seemed convinced I'd never make it to Fort Madison, that I was alive. I wanted to let everyone know I was safe as a bug in a rolling rug.

I pulled the exterior window curtains and plugged my iPad into the electrical outlet on the wall. I slipped in my earbuds. The bed pillows were already propped up behind my back. I settled in to watch a movie, uninterrupted except for pee breaks every to, or the sound of the occasional announcement coming in over the intercom.

Passengers were reminded about safety issues— *Shoes are required at all times*— or pending arrivals— *The next station stop is LaPlata, Missouri.*

On my iPad the opening scene to *Wild* appeared. I'd read Cheryl Strayed's memoir two years earlier and loved it so much I immediately read it again. I'd put off seeing the film version until my journey.

Wild is the story of a woman who attempts an eleven-hundred mile solo hike along the Pacific Crest Trail. It is a tale of triumph and survival over disaster and foolish mistakes. It seemed apropos for my scary-to-only-me solitary adventure.

I leaned back and thought about my trip. *So far, so good.* The first day of traveling alone went fairly well. I didn't have a stroke. My tattoos reminded me to take my medicine on time. I didn't have a headache. My calorie and carb intake were right on track. My knees not only functioned, but I hadn't screamed out in pain, once. Unless I counted the two dollar non-winning Iowa scratch off ticket I'd bought at a gas station along the way, I hadn't lost a dime in gambling.

For me, life didn't get any better than that.

∞

The next station stop is LaMar, Colorado....

The sun peeked through a slit in the curtains as I awoke to the sound of the intercom. The combination of deeply inserted silicone earplugs and a sleep machine that pushed a rush of air through my nasal cavities, blocked out part of the announcement. From what I could gather, the tiny town of LaMar, Colorado would be our next station stop. Breakfast was being served in the dining car and a reservation was not needed.

I looked at the schedule guide my SCA had placed in my room. The train was due to arrive at Lamar at 6:59 a.m. Unfortunately, it was ten minutes after eight. It was only the first morning and the train was over an hour behind schedule.

Seated on my bed, I slipped out of my nightie and slipped on my top with ease. Putting on my pants however, was more of a struggle. I reached under the curtain, unlocked the door and slid it open. With the curtain still pinned together, I managed to step into my pants and hoist them up over my hips, my feet sticking out into the hallway. I put on my required footwear to leave the room, grabbed my purse and makeup and hit the can. I quickly brushed my teeth, took my meds, added a layer of lip gloss and made sure my wig wasn't lopsided.

Except for sleeping, I wear a wig at all times. My lack of hair seems so miniscule in my litany of my physical deficits, I've never written about it. Follicles started disappearing fifteen years ago. I never bothered to find out why. My mother had the same problem. It had to be genetic and I just had to deal with it. Period. One Raquel Welch wig later, I easily walked the streets, holding my head up high.

Breakfast in the dining car is the only meal on Amtrak that doesn't require a reservation. The hours vary but normally it is served between 6:30 a.m. to 9:00 a.m. We were still in the central time zone. Later on in the trip, time zones would become confusing for me. But, I never changed the time on my watch and wouldn't. It was more important that I take my meds at exactly the same time I took them at home. Even in Nevada, I'd be on Central Standard Time.

The Lounge Car Attendant waved me to sit at the first table in the car. Once again I lucked out. I was given an aisle seat. Or perhaps the LCA seated enough obese riders to know the difficulty we large folk had in fitting into the booths. Amtrak dining cars were designed long before the obesity epidemic hit America.

My table came with breakfast companions. One was an extraordinary thin and well-dressed (by Amtrak standards) woman who was traveling across the country alone. She'd grown tired of jetting, she said. Across the table sat a pair of missionaries returning to America after thirty some years in the field.

47

"America's changed," I informed them.

They laughed. The man answered, "We know."

The couple served in a small village in Japan, preaching the gospel and hopefully enjoying sushi. I asked their church affiliation. Religion and I departed ways years ago. The two seemed nice enough, perhaps a bit more polite than any minister and wife I'd yet to encounter. Hopefully, Japanese culture rubbed off on them, instead of the opposite happening.

"Are you going to L.A.?" I asked the single traveler.

Blondie poked at her fruit salad and looked rather uncomfortable, her Botox injected face struggling to display a smile. Perhaps it was my size or obvious lower, economic status that disturbed her. Or maybe she just didn't like Raquel Welch.

Finally, she mumbled back with a forced pleasantry, "Santa Monica."

Ah, that was it! Santa Monica! An ultra rich bitch who must have felt like she was traveling across the country in a cattle car.

I resisted letting out a *moo*.

I turned my attention back to my food, an egg white veggie omelet with a side of apple and maple chicken sausage. I delved in with glee. I estimated the calorie count to be around 400 calories, total. On the last forkful, I noticed the missionaries were studying the tattoos on my hands and forearms.

Almost instantly, I found myself telling a falsehood. With a shrug of my shoulders, I said, "I'm a biker."

The snooty woman next to me slid to her left by another inch or so. The missionary's wife told me to be careful.

Though I am never comfortable with lying, and rarely tell even a tiny fib, I enjoyed the moment. The bike I referred to was my Trek eight-speed that sat in my basement. But my little misdirection allowed the Christian woman to do what she loved to do, give me a pleasant warning of the dangers that lay ahead. I had

48

handed the rich bitch a present as well, another tale of horror to tell at her next Mahjong game. *("Did I tell you darlings about my Amtrak experience? I actually sat next to a ...)*

I scooted back to my room, stopping at the loo along the way. It was 9:15 a.m., and my Kindle was waiting for me. The device contained twenty-seven unread books, along with thirty-seven books I wanted to read again, someday.

As I snuggled into my roomette, I gazed out the big picture window that had become dirty from dirt and dust tossed up into the air by wheels spinning on metal tracks. The scenes of snow covered Missouri had morphed into Midwestern flat lands and wheat fields. A bit later, we'd cross into the ranges of Colorado. I'd watch the sunset across the Arizona desert. The next morning I'd wake up in California, a galaxy away from frozen Minnesota.

But for now, I'd read about travel. Eventually I pulled the curtains shut to reduce the sunlight and clicked on my Kindle. I started to read *Tracks: One Woman's Journey Across 1700 miles of Australian Outback* by Robyn Davison. A truly marvelous book, it had me at the first line ... *"I arrived in Alice at five a.m., with a dog, six dollars, and a small suitcase full of inappropriate clothes."*

If I hadn't been riding my answer to insomnia, I wouldn't have been able to stop until I got to the last page. But once again, the sound of the whistle as the train rocked back and forth had me dozing off almost instantly. Though I had just awoken a few hours earlier from a ten-hour slumber, my eyes closed involuntarily. I was sound asleep by the time the train traveled through the half-mile tunnel at Raton Pass. I woke up just before the last call for lunch.

Albuquerque to L.A.

Arrival in Albuquerque, New Mexico, was an hour and fifty-three minutes late. At 5:05 p.m. I'd been on the train for over twenty-two hours. It was time to breathe fresh air intermingled with train exhaust and the cigarette smoke from dozens of passengers who lit up the moment they stepped onto the platform.

For a girl from Minnesota, the fifty-eight-degree outdoor temperature felt like basking on a tropical beach. I strolled by the rows of Navajo or Zuni vendors. They stood behind tables hawking handmade jewelry, handicrafts, clay pottery, colorful hand woven blankets and area rugs. A used paperback or two made it into their inventory as well. A few years ago I purchased five black beaded necklaces with a pendant for every member of my then writers' group. The necklaces were five bucks each. It only cost me twenty-five dollars to prove I didn't lose all of my money in a casino while on vacation.

Nothing caught my fancy. If it did, I realized I already owned it. Before the conductor called "All aboard," I was seated in the dining car learning how to win a fortune at Roulette from the man sitting next to me.

"Really?" I said nonchalantly, as if I'd heard how to win forty grand every day of my life. "You only need ten bucks to win that amount?"

From the picture window, I could see the tan desert darken as the sun fell below the horizon. Pueblo homes glowed as lights on their inside sent rays of light outward into the night. The New Mexico mountains were behind me. The Southwest Chief was barreling towards Winslow, Arizona where I would not end up standing on a corner with seven women on my mind. The only thing I was concentrating on was what the gentleman in front of me was saying.

"It's true. Roulette is all about maintaining your strategy and betting the same amount, every time," Dan said.

"I thought the game just spun a ball around, or something," a skeptical woman seated next to me said. I'd already heard her life story in a matter of minutes. Helene was a former nun who, in her fifties, discovered the love of her life, an agnostic janitor by the name of Doris.

"That's what people think. But I've won as much as six hundred bucks in one night," he boasted.

"Why not forty grand?" I asked, tasting a bit of my seared Salmon dinner, complete with a chili lime butter sauce and garlic mashed potatoes, (a satisfying 610 calories).

Dan shrugged, his Adam's apple moving up, hampered by the tie he wore. A white shirt and a tie was apparel you rarely saw worn by an Amtrak passenger, but then Dan was an accountant from Kansas City on his way to a convention in Flagstaff. If anyone knew how to keep or lose money, it was a CPA. He answered, "I get bored, easily. Anyway, this is what you need to do ..."

My ears perked up. I'd try to remember what he was about to divulge. But, I'd heard hundreds of sure-fire gambling tips during my decades of debauchery and none of them have worked. I doubted if Dan's would be the one.

He started his explanation, "Say you're willing to lose two hundred bucks?"

"Two hundred dollars?" Helene, the former nun who, for once, was acting like a nun, yelled out.

"Go ahead," I answered, preparing to memorize every word he said. I promised myself that I'd give his strategy a shot when I hit Las Vegas.

By the time dinner was complete and Dan's lecture ended, I shuffled back to my room, exhausted. I fully intended to watch an episode of a BBC mini-drama I'd purchased for the trip. Or at least read another chapter or two of *Tracks*. But like all good intentions, my plans were easily discarded. At 8:00 p.m. I fell sound asleep, only to wake when I hear a booming voice on the intercom say, "Our next station stop will be Union Station, our final destination."

∞

Union Station, the largest depot in the Western United States, is an astonishing blend of Mission Revival, Art Deco, and Spanish/Southwestern architecture. Throughout the decades it has managed to fight off satanic real estate developers proposing demolition or condo conversion.

Perhaps it was the overwhelming perfection of the architecture of Union Station that set me off on a time-travel daydream for a few, brief moments. As soon as the train creaked to a halt, I was decades younger and tens of pounds slimmer. The naturally long, black thick hair of my youth flittered in the wind. The image of a cheap silver colored wig-wearing oversized senior dissolved into an adolescent fantasy of the young Pat running off to Hollywood to become a movie star. I was not sixty-seven but seventeen years of age as I arrived in the land of milk, honey, and Walt Disney.

My feet were swathed in ruby red, four-inch stilettos that could be used to carve a Thanksgiving dinner at Warren Beatty's house, if need be. My pink, thin-strapped dress hinted of both innocence and the possibility of innocence lost rather quickly. My luggage was not the heavy, leather carryall I bought at a thrift store for six dollars in Minnesota, but a red, round vintage American Tourist case. I was the picture of a starlet in waiting.

I paused in the doorway as the make believe scenario paraded across my brain. I inhaled and a California cocktail of sea fed oxygen, train exhaust and smog brought me back to reality in a millisecond.

I stopped my time traveling when I noticed the car attendant shooting an irritated look in my direction. The man's hand was held high in the air, waiting there for me to grab.

Unless I have assistance, there is no way for me at this age and weight to step down from any train safely on my own. Even my size ten, extra wide New Balance shoes with the Velcro straps pulled tightly do not prevent my ability to fall. My steadiness isn't what it used to be. Nor is my common sense.

My sneakers hit the ground and I slipped the attendant twenty bucks for his help for the duration of my trip. For thirty some hours he'd worked hard to keep the sleeping car spotless and the coffee freshly brewed.

He was aware I would be taking the Amtrak bus to Las Vegas. When I'd mentioned that fact a bit earlier, I thought it was my imagination that a look of 'Yikes!' crossed his face. He hailed a Red Cap who steered his electric cart toward us. The driver jumped off and loaded my bags into the back of the vehicle. He asked where I was heading and I answered the Amtrak bus to Las Vegas. Though his face was expressionless it was still able to display his inner thoughts … 'there goes my tip.'

I was beginning to doubt the assurance I'd received two weeks earlier from the Amtrak Reservationist regarding the thruway service. I asked if it provided transportation for Amtrak riders only. She assured me over and over it did.

I wondered if that were actually true, but at that point, what did it matter? My journey was already set in perpetual motion. Nothing was going to stop me from getting to Vegas. Nothing. And besides, how bad could a bus ride be?

The cart, filled now with three other passengers and a dozen bags, weaved through the crowds streaming toward the exits. Overhead, California sunlight began to peek down on the concrete pathway through the open ceiling of metal beams. My fellow passengers were both American snobs and regular folks from across the pond. Each group was heading to different spots throughout the station.

I turned to a frigid woman sitting next to me and said, "Great day, eh?"

She smiled the *'my god why is this old fat lady talking to me?'* smile and turned away. I wondered if she knew the Santa Monica woman and if they were buds.

I turned my attention and ears to the Europeans upfront mentioning movie stars they hoped to encounter when in Los Angeles. Oddly enough, Jim Belushi was on the top of their wish list.

The cart pulled into the landing behind the First Class waiting room. The Europeans stepped off the cart and took their one hundred seventy-four pieces of luggage with them. The snob was still on board. We rode together in silence until she escaped at the stop for the airport shuttle. I didn't even bother to say goodbye.

I was left alone, jiggling about in the hard, cushioned vinyl seat as I basked in the outdoor sun. A few days earlier I'd sat in my living room, watching my husband shovel six inches of snow in our driveway.

In a matter of minutes, the driver sped down a side alleyway next to the station. He ended up at Amtrak's vast parking lot for commercial traffic and public transportation. Dozens of people were already lined up in front of empty bus lanes. The cart swung in the last of four lanes, the one with the Greyhound sign plastered on a concrete column in front of it.

I ask, "Is this the Amtrak shuttle? The one to Vegas?"

He shrugged and responded, "This is where the bus picks you up."

Not a definitive answer for sure. I have a feeling he's endured the same question many times before. I'd have asked him for a clearer, more precise answer but by now, I sounded so much like the snobs I protest about in my daily life I was beginning to hate myself.

What is so wrong about taking a Greyhound, if that is what it turns out to be? How big of a snob was I?

The driver lifted my luggage onto the sidewalk for me. I handed him three bucks for his effort and he gave me a surprised, "Thank you" back.

My inner berating of my hypocritical nature began. *What is so wrong about a Greyhound? Is it because it's filled with poor people? You grew up poor! You grew up with an outhouse. And you were only a few miles from the Chicago city limits! And in your thirties, the only reason your landlord didn't evict you in your thirties is that you ended up marrying him!*

It wasn't traveling with poor people that concerned me. In all of my life experiences on the road as a comedian and in life in general, I have learned that the poorer the person the nicer they are and more giving.

My anxiety wasn't based in elitism. It was an intense awareness of the many stories perpetuated by Hollywood filmmakers and crappy authors. The stereotypical tales that are filled with the usual suspects riding a greyhound bus: a released - by - mistake - only - an - hour - earlier serial killer, an escaped patient from the nearest loony bin, or a life insurance salesman in need of one more sale to meet his quota.

To be brutally honest, my number one issue?

Peeing.

Learning to control one's peeing is a very important life lesson to anyone under the age of three or over the age of sixty.

The nice thing about riding in a sleeper car is there is a restroom on each of the two levels of the car. The one-bedroom compartments have their own personal loo. Rarely have I waited more than a minute or so before relieving my tingling bladder.

If I am in an automobile, I know that a gas station is usually a few minutes away. If need be, I could always pull off the side of the road and squat. Not that I have ever done that, but the comfort in knowing I can, quells any anxiety I have about road travel.

But using a bathroom on a bus? There is a reason my novel *Murder by Chance* begins with a three-hundred and fifty-pound rider found murdered in a restroom on a tour bus. I'm not afraid of being killed, exactly. What I do fear is squeezing into the bathroom and being so obese that I cannot squeeze my way out of it. Of course, I can easily fit into the small space, but my terrors of not being able to fit, are stronger than my realty.

Another debilitating phobia lurks in my consciousness. The locks on the restroom door could jam. I could be trapped inside the moving outhouse for hours until the driver reached his final destination. The driver would resort to using a crowbar to get me free. I would be humiliated when the bladder-deprived passengers gave the driver a round of applause. Me, they'd shoot dirty looks.

Then there is the very true fact that a bit of pee splashing is bound to happen. Once they are in a restroom on a bus, men have to actively hold onto their precious with one hand while their other hand is placed on the wall, trying to secure balance as the vehicle careens down the highway. Statistically, seventy-four percent of the men will miss their mark. Just like they do at home.

I looked at my watch. The bus ride would be between six and seven hours. There was bound to be at least one or two restroom breaks along the way. But, that could be hours away. I glanced at the entrance to the Amtrak station and decided to head for the can one more time. Even though I had just peed fifteen minutes earlier, it would be a prudent measure on my part to try again. If the bus ran according to schedule, I had fifteen minutes to do my deed and get back in time.

I rushed into the station, pulling my luggage behind, my heavy shoulder bag shifting about on my shoulder. The restroom was on the other side of the lobby. A line of women waited outside the entrance. I joined the queue taking note of every second that passed.

I made it back to the departure area just in time to see three newly arrived police cars with their lights spinning and sirens blaring. Bent over one of the police cars was a young man, his hands cuffed behind him. The police performed a quick body search. One of the officers was holding his head firming against the trunk of the car. Four other patrolmen rushed into the station.

I scuffled over to a young man seated on a concrete bench and sat down next to him. An older woman joined us.

"What's up?" I asked.

He shrugged his shoulders, as if witnessing three cops on one citizen was an every day occurrence.

Hector and I became fast friends. Within the first few minutes of meeting him, I'd heard his entire life story, and those of anyone he'd ever met. Hector liked to talk as rapidly as humanly possible. He was a sweet young man with black hair that glistened as much as the thick gold chains that dangled around his muscular neck. His black, silky shorts were loose and reached below his knees. His L. A. Lakers jacket was zipped open, revealing a white, ribbed sleeveless t-shirt.

Hector had a strong Mexican accent though he was born in L.A. He said he grew up in the city but needed to get to Vegas to chill. His friends told him to give it a shot. They claimed he'd love it. Frankly, I couldn't see Hector ever becoming mellow.

He continued his swift dialogue, allowing here and there to let the woman on the other side of me, speak. Living in Tennessee, she was on her way to visit family in San Francisco for the first time. Her connection to Frisco was scheduled to pull into the lane next to Hector's and mine. If nothing else, bus passengers are chatty.

Hector was nonchalant when he asked if I minded if he smoked. I told him to feel free. Why would I care? Within hours I'd be drowning in a tsunami of smoke filled casinos.

Hector reached into his pocket, and instead of pulling out a pack of Marlboros, he removed a plastic container and began to rotate the top to open. My Midwesterner sensibility told me Hector was obviously the frugal sort. He rolled his own cigarettes to save a few pennies. As soon as Hector lit up, the scent told me otherwise.

My jaw dropped open at his brazen, law-breaking attitude. The aging Southern belle and I stared at each with eyes as wide as Hector's pupils. Together, the two of us bolted twenty feet to the left, the furthest we could get away from Hector without standing directly in front of a police car.

"Can you believe …?" I started to ask.

She interrupted. "My family told me to never be surprised by anything in California."

I looked toward the gaggle of cops wondering if one of them had noticed the distinct illegal odor. Hector was such a sweet kid. I didn't want him arrested for his stupidity. I didn't want him to ….

Wait a minute. The plastic bottle Hector kept his weed in was a blue plastic cylinder with a white label encircling it. It was a prescription bottle. Hector was on medical marijuana, perfectly legal in California.

I mentioned that fact to Ms. Tennessee and we humbly headed back to where Hector was sitting. I felt old and outdated as if I'd started a rant about young kids and their music. *Now Jimmy Dorsey! There was a band.*

By now, Hector was quiet and smiling like a contented feline who smoked a dime bag of catnip. We hadn't even left for Las Vegas, yet Hector was already beginning to chill.

Akeisha & The Bus

The bus pulled into a small desert town, an hour or so outside of downtown L.A., and I saw her step off the bus idling next to mine. Akeisha was one of my own. Tribal members fighting the same enemies in the universe. Sadly, the war will never end for either of us. The twenty-some year old warrior was a minimum of one hundred and fifty pounds overweight, maybe even two hundred, or more. Once the weight reaches a certain point, it's hard for me to know.

Her steps were slow, hampered by chubby feet cramped into shoes too small. Her arches looked like a bubble ready to burst. Akeisha was very pretty. Her silky, flowing top and arm full of spangles glittered in the sun. A rhinestone headband circled her head, enveloping the loose ebony curls that highlighted weaves of platinum blonde hair.

Akeisha's make-up sparkled with glitter and even from a distance I could tell she'd carefully outlined her lips into a welcoming heart. Over her shoulder, a crackled pink vinyl tote bag hung filled with whatever. Her tunic was a purplish mixture of complementary colors. Her pants were skintight leggings of a pale mint green. As she swirled around, the cleavage on her backside was as visible as the massive one on her front.

She shuffled in the direction of my bus. I gulped hard and looked at the empty seat next to me. It's not that I didn't want a large person sitting next to me. I understood too well the embarrassment and humiliation that occurs when someone overreacts to having a hefty soul as their seatmate. When I take any public transit I pray I can sit alone. I do not need a single insult, stated or silent, added to my list of perceived wrongs. That fact alone is the reason I prefer a private roomette on a train. No one but me will tell me I do not fit.

I doubted Akeisha and I could fit into the space Greyhound provided for two riders. I'd be overflowing into her designated area as she would overflow both into mine and into the aisle. I'd be scrunched up tightly against the window. As nice as either of us would be to each other, the five-hour plus ride would be unbearable.

As soon as Akeisha climbed on board and began to walk the aisle, purses or bags were instantly placed on seats that were previously empty. She proved herself to be a bright woman. She instinctively knew the drill. She didn't ask anyone to remove items so she could sit down. Instead, she peered hopefully toward the back where I was sitting next to an empty seat.

I had chosen to sit in the second to last row in the aisle. Across from me was a sleeping and very tiny woman who managed to fold herself into a horizontal position, her body huddled within the framework of the two seats. She used the armrest for her pillow. Behind me was a bench seat that could easily fit two people, if not two and a half. It was as wide as two seats and the aisle together. One end butted against the restroom wall. Only one man was sitting on the bench.

Akeisha headed straight to it and said in a sweet tone, "Is the seat next to you taken?"

The thirty-some year old growled, "It's broken. You can't sit here."

"What do you mean it's …" Akeisha started. Her options for seating were becoming limited. Rumors on the Internet state that Greyhound continually oversells the capacity on their buses. If there were no seats for you to sit in, you'd have to wait for the next bus, which in some cases weren't scheduled until the next day. Even then you weren't guaranteed a seat.

"It's broken," he sputtered back as if there were no more questions to be asked. He shoved his bags on top of any unoccupied space.

My '60s styled activist soared into a boil. There was no way the friggin' bench seat could be broken. My head swirled around to protest but Akeisha had already turned her attention to the sleeping woman across from me.

"Ma'am, I need to sit here." Akeisha's tone was firm.

The somnolent sprite lifted up into an upright position. Her spiny fingers rubbed at her eyes before mumbling, "I can go sit with my husband." She scurried out of the seat and walked toward the front. Akeisha breathed a sigh of relief and squeezed in to the small area. She scooted over to the window. She rumbled through her pink tote and pulled out an iPod. She placed the earbuds into her ears, right over her dangling birdcage earrings and looked content. As the bus pulled out, her head bopped up and down in time to the beat of music only she could hear.

I was happy as well. We were forty-five minutes into the trip and Akeisha and I had double seats to ourselves. If we didn't stop at another town, the ride to Vegas would be actually pleasant.

Ten minutes later, the bus veered off the highway once more and pulled into another station. The journey was starting to feel like a metro bus line. I glanced out and saw at least ten people in line. Every seat on the bus would have to be utilized, even the "broken" bench seat behind me.

A young Asian woman ended up sitting next to me. Her small frame barely made a statement in the area that was provided for her. She immediately pulled out a Kindle and started to read. I assumed she was a student. Until I had to go to the restroom and disturb her by asking her to move into the aisle so I could exit, she'd be the perfect seatmate.

Meanwhile, a slim, handsome twenty-some year old man loomed over Akeisha. He wore black jeans and a dark brown t-shirt that looked road weary. He carried a small backpack in his hands.

"Do you mind if I sit?" he asked, his British accent floating through the air like a '90s romance starring Hugh Grant.

Akeisha pulled her earbuds out and beamed a wide, warm smile. "Are you from England?" she gushed before motioning for him to sit.

It was easy to see Akeisha's hormones stirring. Mine would have been as well. The man from across the pond was movie star gorgeous. Still, she looked uncomfortable when he slid into place. It was as if she wanted to apologize for just being alive.

My heart fluttered a bit. It was an apology I, too, had wanted to make most of my life. I sent a prayer upward to my chubby goddess in the sky and asked her to take care of the girl.

Akeisha's friendly seatmate introduced himself. I didn't catch his name but I heard Akeisha proclaim it to be a lovely name. Her voice was as big as her spirit. It easily carried over the sound of the wheels whirling underneath and the continual grind of the engine.

She offered the man a hard candy, but he declined. He must have asked if she'd ever been to Vegas because a conversation began that would last the entire trip. She promised she'd teach him everything he needed to know about Vegas, from where to eat to where to gamble to what shows to see. His gentle laughter proved he was enjoying her well-earned knowledge.

Akeisha announced she was what they called a "high roller." She claimed to always come out a winner. Of course, no one ever believed her, but she insisted it was one hundred and ten percent true.

It wasn't. No one consistently wins in gambling. No one. But the act itself dilutes a player's ability to remember anything but the last time they won. I am convinced Akeisha wasn't lying when she claimed victory over the slots. She was deluded, like all gamblers. She'd continue to believe that statement until her first loss. At that point, all of the losses she'd endured over the years would tidal wave into her consciousness. The disappointments and pain would stay like a polluted oceanfront only to be washed away by the possibility of another tidal wave of a win.

The cycle of lose-win-lose never ends. I know. I have been caught up in it for decades.

I pulled my iPod out of my bag and attached the earbuds. I was preparing to turn it on when the bus pulled abruptly along the side of the highway. My head jolted upwards and I looked around. One thing for sure, it was not a good place to be parked. Cars and semi trucks sped past. The shoulder along the highway was too narrow for a bus.

Upfront, passengers started mumbling. A few minutes later, the gossip finally made it to my ears. The gruff driver had pulled over, not in an emergency, but to make a call to his girlfriend on his cell phone. For five minutes he continued to chat away while passengers in the back began making bets when we'd be jackknifed by a semi.

As one last truck passed at a speed close to a near death experience, the driver abruptly pulled back on the highway and sped off.

Relieved, I placed the earbuds back in my ears and turned on my iPad. A few weeks earlier, I'd downloaded a video of a three-hour British miniseries entitled *The Secret of Crickley Hall*. The series was based on James Herbert's bestselling ghost story. I'd actually already watched a bit of it on the train. It was an enjoyable spine tingler. The episodes were an hour each. If I focused on the first one, perhaps I could make it through an entire hour before I had to get up to pee.

The credits were running across the screen fifty-eight minutes later when I had no choice but to use the restroom. How bad could it be? I'd only seen a few brave souls enter the forbidden land.

I caught my seatmate's attention and pointed to the restroom. She immediately stood up and stepped out of my way. I took a few steps into the aisle and opened the restroom door. I held my breath as soon as the urine stench hit my nostrils and stepped inside the cramped space.

I was, however, relieved I fit inside the lavatory. The floor was a sheet of ridged stainless steel. The toilet was also steel. The wall material was comprised of a greyish plastic or fiberglass. I had the distinct feeling I was heeding nature's call inside a prison cell. Fortunately, the floor wasn't sticky. That was a very good sign.

Because I am a coward, I didn't dare look into the toilet before I sat on it, nor did I actually sit on it. I grabbed a bunch of toilet paper and wiped the seat clean. I tossed the paper inside the bowl. Unless we hit a speed bump and I fell backward, no way would I let any part of my body touch anything. I managed to hunch my corpulent self over the hole and heard the sound of tinkles. I've never peed so fast in my life.

When I finished I realized there wasn't a sink but a gigantic bottle of hand sanitizer attached to the wall. When I hit the button to let a stream of gunk fall into my palm, the button didn't work. Nothing shot out of it.

I exited the room and squeezed back into my seat. I grabbed the travel size bottle of Purell from my carryall bag. I squirted the chemically pine-scented liquid into my palms and vowed not to use the bus restroom again. Though it actually hadn't been that bad of an experience, there was no telling what the next experience could be like. Frankly, I didn't want to find out.

I leaned back in my seat and heard Akeisha tell her Brit that Circus Circus was actually a classy hotel and casino, though a lot of people didn't agree with her. There were acrobats and jugglers who performed free-of-charge. You could spend all day watching them twirl about, just in case you'd already lost your money on the machines. And Slots of Fun, next door, sold foot long hotdogs for ninety-nine cents, just in case he was interested.

I clicked on the second episode of Crickley Hall. Ten minutes after I'd finished it, the driver announced we were pulling into Barstow for a 15-minute break.

Thank God. I would be able to make it to an actual restroom without peeing myself.

Maybe.

∞

The stop in Barstow sits along good old Route 66, a highway filled with old timers and tourists trying to get their kicks on. There is no way humanly possible not to begin humming the infamous tune the moment you see signs along the side of the road. In reality, the ditty is basically just a listing of towns along the way from Chicago to L.A., and not even presented in the correct geographical order. If you drove it the same way they sing it, you'd have to circle back a few times along the way.

Recording artists from Arrowsmith to The Rolling Stones recorded their own version of the song. However, the only voice I choose to remember is that of Nat King Cole as the Greyhound slid to a halt.

The bus depot and surrounding buildings, were a conglomerate of shops and fast food places including a Popeye's Fried Chicken, McDonalds, Subway, Panda Express, Dunkin Donuts, fudge shops, Darigold Ice Cream, Subway, Starbucks, Barstow Station Liquor, retail shops, postcard vendors and more. Not only were Greyhound buses paused, but truckers, bikers and carloads of hungry, bladder busting tourists also congregated.

Barstow lies one hundred fifteen miles from Union Station in Los Angeles and one hundred fifty miles from Las Vegas. Not exactly halfway, but close enough for my bladder to do its happy dance upon arrival.

The grumpy driver barked, "Okay folks. This is a fifteen-minute break. Not a minute longer. I don't care if you're back on the bus or not, I am leaving on time. And that fifteen minutes begins," he takes the time to dramatically look at his wristwatch, "now."

Though I really wanted to bolt to the front and make a beeline to the restroom, that action wasn't a possibility. There were fifty some passengers in front of me. Every single one was getting off the bus, slowly. I calculated my odds for making it back to the bus in time for departure. Including the likely scenario of standing in line at the lavatory, I'd be hitchhiking to Vegas.

A Popeye restaurant stood on the opposite side of the parking lot. A few of the bus riders were headed in that direction. I knew I couldn't make that within the allotted time. My gait is painfully halting. No one who possessed a shred of literary ability would describe what I do as walking. Lumbering is a more accurate description.

By the time I stepped off the bus, I opted to go into the Barstow Station, even if that meant climbing up ten steps to get inside.

Steps and stairs are not my friends, not with these knees. A victim of a botched up knee surgery and subsequent aging has me avoiding stairs whenever possible. When I do walk up or down them, it is one step at a time, each leg firmly positioned on a single step before I can attempt the next. If I were cast as an extra in a disaster movie, I'd be the old lady crushed to death by the fleeing crowd.

After searching for any handicap entrance or ramp, I relented and slowly climbed the steps into the building. Once inside, the situation looked grim. Dozens, of customers spanned the horizon in front of me. They gathered in long lines in front of fudge displays, ice cream vendors and racks of t-shirts with Route 66 blazoned across the front.

An arrow shaped sign on a wooden stairwell caught my eye. It pointed up to a third level that looked more like a storage area. Normally, I'd avoid any level that wasn't accessible by an escalator. Yet, at that moment, I made a bold decision. I'd rather risk injuring my knees climbing stairs than peeing my pants.

The upper facility was not the main restroom, but it was one I might be able to actually use before racing back to the bus in slow motion. I hobbled up the steps and made it to the landing. A line wasn't snaked around to the lady's room. I was the only one who chose to climb the stairs.

I did what had to be done and headed back down to the main floor. I gave up the idea of purchasing a snack. I was too terrified of being stranded. I made it back to my seat within four minutes of departure.

Thirty seconds later, Akeisha returned carrying a large paper bag of Popeye goodies and an extra large drink. Her seatmate was nowhere to be seen. She snuggled near the window and pulled out what looked like a wrapped Po' Boy sandwich. One bite and waves of ecstasy engulfed her shining face. Akeisha managed to take one more munch before her Brit returned and she slid the Po' Boy back into the bag. For the rest of the trip, she'd occasionally reach inside the paper bag and grab a bit of the sandwich with her hands and place it discretely in her mouth.

Akeisha was likely a secret eater, just like I have been most of my life. I still remember when I was twenty-something and a friend said he didn't understand why I was fat. He never saw me eat, not a single bite. We'd been friends for over two years.

The bus driver climbed back on board, and without even bothering to do a head count, or look back at the passengers to see if they were all there, he started the engine and sped off.

I turned my attention to the second installment of *The Secrets of Crickley Hall*. By the time it was over, the bus was speeding past the town of Primm, Nevada.

We were forty miles from Las Vegas. I shut off the video. I was too excited to do anything but stare out the window to catch sight of billboards, one after the other promising star-studded entertainment, fabulous food and the possibility of a fortune just up the road.

Before I left Minnesota, I'd downloaded every possible song I could find that had a connection to Vegas for me. The first song on my play list was *Holiday Road* from the movie *Vegas Vacation*. After that, *Born To Be Alive*, a petty disco era song from Patrick Hernandez blasted my ears. The one-hit wonder seemed more than appropriate for a road song. Hitting the jackpot one time—the big one, that is—and then walking away from gambling forever, is pretty much every gambler's secret dream.

The only problem with that big jackpot though is, it is never big enough.

By the time we neared the city limits, Kanye West's "*Can't Tell Me Nothing*" lyrics 'La la la wait till I get my money ...' had me dancing in my seat.

It seemed like an omen that as soon as the Welcome to Las Vegas sign came into view, Elvis sang the last bar of Viva Las Vegas. I clicked off my iPod. I didn't need to listen to road music anymore. After two thousand miles of travel, I'd reached my destination.

Day One: Vegas

The bus arrived in Downtown Las Vegas at 6:40 p.m. Unlike McCarran airport there were no taxis waiting at the Greyhound station to transport pilgrims to hotels and casinos throughout the city. Nor were there any shuttle vans filled with giddy and anxious passengers. The assumption seemed to be that a Greyhound rider would do one of two things—take public transit or walk.

The driver yanked my bags out of the luggage compartment and tossed them on the ground. I bit into my lip in order to suppress an urge to cuss at him. Getting on a Homeland Security watchlist was not in my best interest. The TSA, by law, has to listen to any lunatic driver's delusional rant concerning any passenger they deem inappropriate.

Rescuing my bags from the stacks, I trudged two blocks to the back of the Golden Nugget Hotel. For the next three nights, I'd stay on the strip at the Excalibur, a seven-mile cab ride away.

Several taxis waited near the entrance of the Golden Nugget, the only four-star establishment in Downtown Vegas. I climbed into one and mumbled "Excalibur, please" and crossed my fingers. Taking a cab ride in Las Vegas is always a risk.

Check on any travel forum about Vegas and you'll find a main topic of concern is being taken advantage of by a cab driver. Whether it is being driven through the infamous "tunnel" to or from the airport, thereby adding another fourteen dollars or so to the cost; or adding thirty minutes to the time by driving down the jam-packed Strip.

As always, I decided that if I ended up being screwed, it's always better to know who was doing the screwing.

"How long have you been a driver?" I asked, wondering if he would head down Las Vegas Boulevard or jump onto the expressway. Of course, there was the possibility he might take the much saner and cheaper route of Dean Martin Drive.

"Twenty-seven years," he answered, veering onto Dean Martin.

Cha ching! Score! I was a winner already!

"Wow," I said. "That's a long time. You born here?"

No one ever is.

He answered, "New Delhi."

We continued in silence while we drove past Akeisha walking down the street, pulling her luggage behind her, tottering dangerously on her high heels.

"How's business?" I asked.

"Slow," he answered.

They always say that.

He didn't bother to ask where I was from, nor did he seem interested in talking, though he was a pleasant enough fellow. We passed behind the Fashion Show Mall, Treasure Island, The Mirage, Caesar's, Bellagio and continued southward. We were headed to the Excalibur where us poorer folk congregate to gamble, pray and play. My destination may have been the reason my driver chose the cheapest route.

We pulled into the back entrance of the Excalibur. The fare from downtown was fourteen bucks. I gave the driver a twenty and told him to keep the change. I limped inside, past rows of slot machines until I finally stood in front of registration. Twenty guests were in the queue and five clerks were working behind the desk. It took only a few minutes before I was heading to the twenty-first floor of Tower One. Over the years, my fear of heights had lessened to allow me to stay on higher floors in hotels, especially if they were in Las Vegas. My gambling obsession turned out to be stronger than any of my anxieties.

I stepped out and followed the directional arrows on the wall. My room was at the very end of the corridor, located right next to the stairwell. It is a room we in the mystery writer biz call *The Murder Room*. If you're going to kill someone staying in a hotel, the room at the end of the hall is the perfect place. The stairwell made for easy access and an easier escape.

I gave it little regard, figuring it was more important I burn off calories walking the long length of the hall. Besides, weren't there security cameras all over the casino? Or at least that is what I had always heard. I wasn't worried in the least.

Now looking back on it, I should have been.

By the time I unpacked, it was 7:00 p.m. and I was starving. I struggled a bit about the sanity of leaving my room when I was that tired. It would be cheaper for me to order a thirty-buck meal from room service then to chance walking across a gaming floor.

My opting for sanity lasted around fifteen seconds. Within minutes, I was riding in the elevator on a quest for nourishment, vowing not to gamble. Not even a penny. Surely, I could resist the urge to wager and be happy with filling my gut? After all, I had a detailed—to the penny—plan. It wouldn't be like that one disastrous vacation when Circus Circus ate up a grand in a matter of hours on the very first day, half of my spending allowance for the entire week. I was wiser now. My funds were paper clipped together in daily bundles.

How could I ever justify spending more?

Two hours later, I was a bit heavier from eating a grilled shrimp chili lime salad from Baja Fresh but my wallet was extremely lighter—by three hundred and twenty dollars.

It was going to be a long week.

Day Two: Vegas

At 6:00 a.m. sounds of raucous laughter stirred me out of my slumber. After a night of partying, a gaggle of young women stood congregated in the hallway. The hooting and hollering echoed through the walls and under the door. I stumbled to the peephole to view the giggling bachelorette party. The soon-to-be bride's ensemble included streams of packaged condoms pinned to her skintight dress, a few of the rows shorter than the others. A wad of currency stuck out of her cleavage. A pre-wedding tradition for the Vegas bride-to-be is that she and her bridesmaids sell condoms for any price they can get at the nearest bar. One young woman told me she'd once received a hundred bucks for one condom. Others said most of the men they pleaded with made a buck donation. A few of the women said they were offered additional money if they'd include slipping the rubbers on the purchasers. A couple of the drunker ones did.

The ladies across the hall were so inebriated they could only stand upright in a huddle, holding on to each other as they fell into their room.

It was Good Friday, Las Vegas style.

I walked into the bathroom and hit the red button on the electric water pot I had brought with me. I'd filled the pot with water the night before, as well as laid out the foldable coffee filter and a container of finely ground coffee. Within a few minutes I was sipping my daily mud. Like any good addict, I travel with my drug of choice and the necessary paraphernalia needed for its consumption.

Vegas hotel rooms do not offer coffee pots … not unless it's a suite and even then it's highly unlikely. The last time I checked, a pot of room service coffee was twenty-two bucks a pop and if you wanted a second cup for your roommate it was an additional nine dollars.

After I finished my first cup, indulged in a long shower, perused my email and checked out the local news stations, I decided to count my stash of cash.

Like most gamblers, I use creative accounting when it comes to gambling. For instance, the money spent at Diamond Jo's in Iowa didn't figure into my vacation gambling budget, not one penny of it. Because my husband rode along for that portion of the trip, I considered it a "family" trip and therefore did not have to be held accountable for any money I may or may not have lost.

My budget for Vegas included seven days of gambling, entertainment and food for a total of twenty-one hundred dollars, roughly three hundred dollars a day. Over two frickin' grand! That is a huge amount of money if you don't gamble—and a ridiculously small amount if you do, especially if you travel two thousand miles to wager.

My hotel fees didn't figure into my Vegas budget. Because of the free room offers sent via email and various players' discounts my hotel cost for the entire eight nights was a total of $387.00. I'd worry about paying that credit card charge later, after I returned home. Right now, all I had to be concerned with was staying within my daily cash allotment.

My husband and I are like kids when it comes to money. We each get a monthly allowance which we can do with as we please. Anything over that has to be accounted for at a family meeting, which we usually manage to put off until the next month, month after month.

Because I prefer to keep my gambling expenditures private, and thereby lessen the chance for lectures, I save up all year for my annual gambling trip.

A portion of my allowance and profits from selling my junk on eBay are added to it. Therefore, when I lose in a single week the two grand it took me a year to accumulate, I still feel like a moron, but a frugal one.

I can gamble on one twenty-dollar bill for ten hours—or I can lose it in a matter of minutes. It all depends upon the luck of the machines. My hope for Vegas was to be able to carry over my stash from one day's allowance to the next. I had six hundred dollars cash to start with, almost all of it hidden in my homemade bra safe.

If I were lucky, that amount would last me the entire trip. I wouldn't have to wait in line at an ATM before pressing accept when asked if I agreed to the eight dollar withdrawal fee. Again, not a typo. Any fee is higher in Vegas. Don't bother to ask why. It just is.

I decided to devise a food plan for the day. I was serious about staying on my grain, gluten and sugar-free diet. I'd managed to do it on the train with no problem. Now that I was actually in Vegas, it would take a bit more determination and strategy.

Buffets appeared to be my best bet. They offered a large salad bar with all the fixings, fresh fruits, cooked veggies and an abundance of grilled or roasted meat, poultry or fish. There was little chance of starvation.

My plan was to skip breakfast every day and have a massive lunch followed by a tiny dinner. But because it was a holiday, I decided my very first full day in Vegas eating would be different. Holiday eating in Vegas can be a bit scary and time consuming.

One Thanksgiving in Las Vegas, my husband and I waited in line an hour and twenty minutes at the Wynn Buffet. We paid an additional fifteen bucks on top of their forty-five dollar charge for dinner to be admitted to priority seating. Those who didn't pay the additional surcharge waited three to four hours to be seated. The buffet at the Wynn is just that good.

So on my first morning in Vegas—Good Friday— my plan was to load up on a big breakfast at the hotel.

Later, I'd have a light lunch and dinner purchased at a fast food joint that offered salads.

Unfortunately, on my way to The Buffet at the Excalibur, I couldn't resist stopping at an *Iron Man* penny slot. The image of Robert Downey, Jr. splashed across the machine called to me. I slid a five-dollar bill into the slot just to say hello. Within a matter of minutes I was down twenty-two bucks. Oh well. At least Robert would understand. Downey is a man who knows a thing or two about addiction.

Once inside The Buffet, there were only a few patrons at the tables, maybe twenty or so. The hostess instructed me to find a table on my own. As soon as I sat, a server laid utensils in front of me. She pointed out the beverage service area where I could get coffee or juice. A mimosa or Bloody Mary would be an extra charge. She offered to retrieve the booze-laden drinks.

I shook off her offer and headed straight to the food station. I grabbed a plate and piled it high with scrambled eggs. I passed over the offerings of huevos rancheros or eggs benedict. Unlike higher end buffets, Excalibur didn't offer an omelet station where I could order one made to my exact liking.

Next, I added two sausage patties and three slices of crisp bacon. Wedges of cantaloupe and melon were added with a heaping tablespoon of salsa verde for my scrambled eggs. Though it was breakfast, a hearty Asian offering of sushi and noodles stood by. I stuck with my American styled breakfast. I waddled to the beverage bar and filled a cup of coffee and managed to carry both plate and mug back to my table. Had it been one of my many bad knee days, I couldn't have done either and would have chosen a sit-down restaurant. But, Vegas is all about excess and nothing says over the top like an all-you-can-stuff-into-your-mouth buffet.

I ate in silence, planning the rest of my day. I would take the free tram from Excalibur to Mandalay Bay, and then work my way back through the Luxor, Excalibur, and ending up at my favorite casino for gambling: New York-New York. It is the one casino where the Vegas magic happened to me, once. I've been chasing the same experience ever since.

My goal was to experiment with a YouTube project I'd announced on Facebook. I am a big fan of YouTube. I can easily spend an afternoon perusing everything from tiny houses to tiny hamsters living in tiny houses eating tiny pizzas while sitting on tiny furniture in tiny outfits. I am more easily entertained by some housewife in Yuma than I am by phony Hollywood stars.

I also watch gambling videos, specifically live play slot videos. Unless you're an addicted slot player like I am, or a really old lady with nothing to do, watching a live play slot will literally make you hang yourself in boredom.

But I, and hundreds of thousands of other viewers, enjoy the vids. I feel they give me an edge, understanding how the different slot games work and their different bonuses or payoff features. The best of the videos have lively commentators who bemoan their losses or loudly celebrate their wins. Many of them engage in high stakes gambling at ten, twenty or one hundred dollars a spin. Others, like me, concentrate on the lowest possible bet, twenty-five or forty cents.

The category called Live Play Videos involves live gambling for a specific time or money amount. I decided to combine both. I'd slip a twenty-dollar bill into every casino on the strip and video it. I'd gamble for five minutes max or until my twenty was history. Then I'd move onto the next casino and do the same. Twenty-nine casinos at twenty dollars a pop equaled five-hundred-and-eighty dollars wagered. My own mini-series of mini wagers.

Unfortunately, my planned scenario had a few possible hiccups I'd have to address, like the fact that casinos generally do not allow videotaping or cameras. Before the onslaught of camera phones, warning signs were posted on every entrance. No camera or recording devices allowed! Security guards would not only stop you from taking a photo but often asked you to leave the premises. A few have been known to confiscate the equipment in order to assure other gamblers' privacy. Jackpots were often denied when a casino discovered the play had been videotaped.

The privacy of any player was one of the reasons rules against cameras were put into place. Grandpa Joe may not want the world to know he's sitting at a slot machine gambling his kid's inheritance. But in this age of cellphone cameras, casinos often turn a blind eye, perhaps realizing that vacation videos are free advertising. Still, the thought of being caught while I taped didn't sit lightly with me.

My other concern was my inept skills with my iPod, the only device with a camera I carried. The only videos I'd ever taken were a few of my husband as he sat at the dining room table telling me to turn the camera off. In only one of them did I manage to capture his entire head. I hadn't a clue how to save the video or send it to "The Cloud", whatever that is.

If this is a bit confusing, just picture your great-grandmother trying to figure out a Samsung television remote. That's exactly the level of tech savvy I possess.

I swallowed the last of the coffee, left a few bucks for the server and headed out of the restaurant. I angrily scurried past the *Iron Man* slot where I'd lost twenty-two bucks earlier. Briefly, I wondered if I could win it back. A part of my brain views a slot machine as a sofa, and all of the money I've lost over the years is hidden somewhere in the crevices.

"Hey young lady, would you like a photo taken with me?" a baritone voice called out.

I bristled. I hate it when anyone calls me a young lady. It is an insult to my intelligence. It's as if a salesman thinks I will buy whatever he is selling because he pretends he thought I was younger than I look. Preparing to let out a rant, I swung around and realized there was no need. The young man who said it possessed the intelligence of a dust particle. He was the perfect example of a steroid enhanced Bimbro.

The Bimbro stood next to another dancer from Excalibur's production of *Thunder From Down Under*, Australia's version of the Chippendale dancers. He and his bud were tanned, muscular and smiling through a set of gleaming pearly whites. Tight black leather pants caressed their bodies, enhancing every ripple and bulge. The only things on their expanded chests were gold chains and sweat. For a brief moment my aging body forgot its continuing decay and managed to locate the last remaining drop of estrogen.

I almost said, "Oh wow!" out loud.

I declined their offer of posing for a photo for my "mates" back home. Nor did I succumb to solicitation by another pair of over-the-top sexual beings. Two nearly naked women offered an additional photo op. They wore pink short shorts that rode above their butt cheeks and a miniscule bra made of an industrial strength material to hold their enormous, silicone enhanced breasts. White fluffy bunny ears wiggled about on their heads. Their feet were encased in pearl-colored stilettos. The duo jumped up and down, their hands held in paw like positions, enticing everyone who passed to take an "Easter photo for your basket." More than a few groans of desire came from men who were thrilled with their intentional euphemism.

I exited out of the Excalibur and ended up on a landing where I could choose walking across a bridge to New York-New York or taking the free tram ride to Luxor and Mandalay Bay. I opted for the tram. Ten minutes or so later, I stepped off onto Mandalay Bay property. I headed down the long hallway toward the casino, passing dozens of shops and eclectic vendors along the way. Every inch of Las Vegas real estate is designated for one purpose only—making money.

At the south end of the strip Mandalay Bay sits as a tribute to all things golden. The forty-three-story hotel and casino, sitting on one hundred twenty acres glistens boldly on the desert landscape. Every window is tinted gold and held up by white beams of steel. The interior of the complex reinforces the feel of wealth. Touches of gold are everywhere from the floors to the ceilings. The casino is light and airy. Unlike so many of the old school interiors for gaming, Mandalay Bay's openness is a welcome relief to the old school of thought that believes gamblers prefer doing their dirty deeds in the dark.

I cruised the slot aisles before deciding to sit at a penny slot. I pulled out my twenty and my iPod. But I suddenly realized I was sitting directly on the center aisle. Not a good place to be if I wanted to remain hidden from security.

I skittered down a few rows and found a DaVinci Diamonds penny slot machine. I slipped in my dough, turned on my iPod and hit record. Or I thought I hit record. I didn't know for sure. I regretted the decision to "learn as I go" in Las Vegas. I basically had no idea what I was doing.

I looked into the viewfinder and noticed the machine shaking. Thankfully, it wasn't an earthquake, though it looked like it. My hands were trembling. I was that nervous about being caught. I feared not only getting banned from a casino, but having security confiscate my iPod, or delete the contents.

I peered around me, wondering if I was being noticed. I hit the play button again and fifty cents disappeared into the universe. Crap. I was already down a dollar.

I continued playing. In three minutes time I spent the twenty. Not a bonus to be had. My brain calculated the total I was down for the trip, three hundred eight-three dollars. My mind shifted into a less depressing mode. I discarded yesterday's memory of the money I lost on my dinner quest. So far, that morning I'd only gambled forty-two dollars. I didn't bother to add in the twenty-one dollars for breakfast.

That sounded a lot better, even if in reality I'd only gambled for a total of thirty minutes.

Shit, I mumbled out loud, realizing they were the very first words I recorded. So much for my including a clever and witty audio. The whole point of the video was for me to be rambling on in a humorous way while throwing in a reference or two to my books available online for purchase.

Right now, the only thing I uttered on the video was a swear word, and a pathetic one at that.

Feeling frustrated, I left Mandalay Bay and headed toward the Luxor. The Excalibur, Luxor and Mandalay Bay resorts are connected by a vast corridor of shopping, restaurants, and clubs. I didn't bother getting back on the tram.

Luxor, with its thirty-story black pyramid and its gigantic golden sphinx sitting in front of the entrance is one of the most photographed icons on The Strip. Kitsch was in style when the Egyptian tribute was built. The onyx-hued property sits next to a medieval castle that sits across the street from a faux replica of the New York City skyline, complete with a functioning roller coaster zipping around the perimeter.

When I reached the Luxor gaming floor, I ended up sitting at *The Bridesmaids'* slot machine. Melissa McCarthy's face beamed at me, as well as other stars of the raunchy film. I have this unproven theory that slots connected to celebrities rarely pay off, as the slot machine manufacturers needed to pay royalties to the celebrities as well as the casino. However, my hypothesis has never stopped me from playing a star themed slot, especially, if I like the movie star as much as I like McCarthy. Melissa is a great example of a big girl making it really big.

I slipped in my twenty and fumbled around again with my camera. I noted the time: 11:37 a.m. At 11:42, I'd either be richer, poorer or even. Three spins later I hit the bonus round.

"Woo-hoo!" I yelled rather weakly, hoping the audio on the camera picked up the sound. I was not only afraid of attracting attention but my energy level was close to zero. In comedy, the most important ingredient is energy. No one wants to listen to a video with a narrator who sounds like that old lady in the Titanic Movie.

Really? James Cameron? What were you thinking?

The *Bridesmaids* slot bonus round I won was the Bridal Gown Showdown. Many of the slot games like *The Bridesmaids* are interactive, alluding to a false sense of control as you chose which image to press, which button to move, which question to answer. If you lose it's because you've chosen the wrong move. If you win, it's because you're a genius.

Check any of the gambling slot forums and you'll find out that most of the results of a computerized game are often pre-determined. It's not like the old days, when the spin of a mechanical wheel determined your destiny. Now it is in the hands of the game designing IT folks.

In the film, a luncheon at a Brazilian steak house leads to a major bout of food poisoning, complete with all the disgusting side effects. Ditto the slot game.

I chose which skewer to slide onto a plate in front of each actress using my finger to do so. My food choice decision would be either good or really bad. Eventually, all the women on the screen become ill, just like in the movie. Except this time, you get credits for killing them off slowly.

When the bonus round ended, I was up $11.22. I clicked off my iPod camera and debated whether to leave. I was up a bit, and my goal was just to tape in each casino. Theoretically, I could leave, but heck, I was ahead. Maybe I could win a bit more, maybe win back that money lost at the *Iron Man* ....

I hit play and I felt my shoulder being rubbed hard. A firm pair of hands pressed firmly into my flesh while a female voice said. "You lucky."

I didn't bother to turn around. If you win a jackpot or even a bonus, you're considered "lucky" by other gamblers. No one bothers to consider the fact that you may have already lost one thousand dollars a few minutes earlier. All they know is for that moment the gambling gods are smiling down on you. And if they touch you, the luck might be contagious.

I've been rubbed harder in casinos than at any massage parlor. And the only happy ending in sight is the sound of fake coins falling into a fake metal bin.

"Yeah," I acknowledged. "I am lucky."

"You playing long time?" she asked.

"A few minutes," I replied. "I'm leaving. You can have the machine if you want." It was close to lunchtime. I was hungry and the New York-New York food court was calling my name.

I exited the gaming floor of the Luxor and continued through the hallway that connected it to Excalibur. I found the main entrance again, but this time I didn't head to the tram station. Instead I took a turn to the left and walked across the bridge that spanned Tropicana Avenue. Once on the other side there are only two choices. Take the escalator or elevator to the street level or walk directly into the second level of New York, New York with its shops and fast food joints.

Once inside, I located the escalator to the gaming floor and headed down. But for a change, I didn't rush to the slots. I went directly to the food court, one of the nicest in Las Vegas. But it wasn't the delis that attracted me. It was the one Las Vegas casino where magic had happened to me. The one casino where within one hour I had won enough money to pay for our trip, to give my husband a thousand dollars, take a grand for myself, and still have tons of money left over to gamble.

Magic

It had happened on my sixteenth trip to Las Vegas. Before that, my visits would have me losing every dime or, if I were lucky, breaking even. Never did I walk away a winner, clutching thousands of dollars in my hands. Or better yet, holding onto a check for millions of dollars like Elmer Sherwin did, twice.

Ninety-two-year old Elmer won 21.1 million dollars at the Cannery in North Las Vegas. Sixteen years earlier, in 1989, he won 4.6 million at the Mirage. When interviewed about his second mega win, he said his dream was to "win big twice."

For a true gambler, once is never enough.

I never dreamt about hitting the big one, because for me it wasn't possible. Playing the lowest bet allowed on any machine eliminated the possibility of scoring the big payoff. Normally, you're not in the running unless you play the max bet.

Being the frugal gambler I am meant I'd have to quit playing early because my money would run out sooner. Keeping in the action, for me, is more important. I simply love to play and never think about winning or losing. I claim I'd be just as thrilled with a four or five-thousand dollar win as I would with a million.

And son of a gun, I was.

∞

Even on vacation, my husband and I follow a strict schedule. Every morning we'd stop by the ATM in the hotel lobby. I'd withdraw our maximum daily limit, three hundred bucks. My husband would take one hundred and I'd keep the rest. With luck, it would take me all day to lose the two C's.

We'd immediately head to the pool and bake in the sun. After an hour, I'd leave my husband alone, gifting him the chance to ogle in peace. Later, at 5:00 p.m., we'd meet in our room to plan our evening.

For six hours, I'd wander the strip alone, moving from casino to casino placing one forty-cent wager after another. I'd start out the day by slipping twenty bucks in a machine. The twenty would be lost fairly quickly. In disgust, I'd head to the closest casino, the Bellagio. Or I'd cross the street and try my luck at Casino Royale.

Once there, because I'd already lost twenty dollars, I'd hit the cashier's cage to exchange the nine twenties for eighteen ten dollars bills. I'd slip a ten into the first slot … and soon …. well … I'd be at the next casino, trading in my tens for fives.

On that one day of magic, my losing streak stayed with me for hours. By 1:00 p.m. when I walked into New York-New York, I had only five bucks in my pocket. My schedule called for four more hours of gambling. I'd never make it that far. I was sure I'd run out of cash within a matter of minutes.

My luck was bound to change, I'd tell myself over and over. It wasn't *fair* I couldn't find a single winning machine.

The one personality characteristic that reaches across the gambling community is a belief that life should be fair.

Because if it is, one day you'll get yours.

84

I walked carefully around the New York-New York gaming floor. I knew that when my last penny was spent, I'd head back to my hotel room in shame. Eventually, I'd contact my husband. I'd text him one word … hungry. He'd rush back and escort me to the nearest buffet to drown my sorrows with carved turkey and blueberry pie.

Afterwards, we'd end up at the half price ticket booth and catch the cheapest show still available. Any gambling I'd do would have to wait until the next morning, when I hit up the ATM once again.

But this time it was different.

I slipped the five-dollar bill into a Triple Seven machine, a gutsy move on my part. I never played dollars slots, ever. But if I was going to burn out in a matter of minutes, I decided to do it in blaze of glory.

I pressed play and the wheel spun around. Two white sevens appeared, and then nothing. I hit it again. Nada. On the third try, with two bucks left in the machine, One seven appeared, and then another, and then … a third.

The lights flashed, bells went off. A siren came out of nowhere. I'd won one thousand dollars.

"Good for you," the man sitting next to me said between puffs on his stinky cigar. "People have been losing all day on that machine."

I smiled weakly at him. I was in such shock, I couldn't talk. If I had had any sense, I would cash out and walk away. The thousand dollars would cover the cost of Steve's plane ride, our meals, our hotels—an almost free vacation.

I vowed one more time to stop and quickly realized the futility of my words. Quicker than instantly, I decided to let myself spend another hundred, and that would be it. I'd still leave with nine hundred bucks in my pocket.

I started playing again, one dollar at a time—and after losing thirty-nine times in a row, son-of-a-gun—I did it again.

Three red sevens lined up in front of me. One thousand dollars again! I nearly fell off my chair.

"Jesus Christ," my neighbor guy muttered, barely able to contain his anger at his own misfortune. "I knew I should've switched seats."

There would be no more congratulations or camaraderie aimed in my direction. It was best that I move quickly away from him.

Clutching the stack of bills in my hand, my eyes scanned the area. I spotted an *I Dream of Jeannie* nickel machine. I slid a twenty-dollar bill into the slot, then two more. The $1,900 I won in a matter of minutes could easily be lost as quickly. It only took a few more minutes of play for me to be down to $1,840.

Then I hit again.

This time it was only $450.

Only $450????? Was I becoming so delusional or greedy that an amount I would have once been overjoyed with winning had become an *only?*

My pot had surged back over two grand. I continued to play on various machines. By the end of forty minutes there was $2800 inside my zippered purse. I was giddy with glee to the point of hyperventilating. It couldn't get any better.

But of course it did.

On the very next press of the button, I hit my biggest win of the day—$1199.00. I began to feel as if nothing could stop me. Nothing. Except for the two casino workers headed my way.

We gamblers are not only superstitious but we're gullible, believing every rumor we've heard in regards to winning or losing. The legend of "the cooler" begins with the unproven theory that casinos hire unlucky individuals who spread negative vibes wherever they go. Good luck instantly turns bad for anyone unfortunate enough to be near them.

Whether these two cheerful women were coolers or not, I noticed I started to lose as soon as they stood next to me, gabbing away. If they weren't professional downers, they were definitely a distraction. That alone was reason enough for the powers to be to send them to see what was really going on.

Now, if I'd won, say thirty grand at one machine, that little act would not have created such attention. But winning a jackpot at one machine after another was suspicious. That just didn't happen.

But it was happening to me and I had no clue why. I wasn't using a metal "money paw" on a slot machine to tinker with the insides. Nor had I cruised eBay to buy an electronic gadget guaranteed to trigger a win. As far as I knew Jupiter was not in my fifth house, whatever that meant. I only remembered my friend, who dabbled in astrology, told me to make sure it was every time I gambled.

Nor was I a fortuneteller. Never did I stroll up to a machine and see myself winning. If I did see anything, it was always me losing. But for some reason, I was on a roll, winning jackpot after jackpot.

And nothing scares a casino more.

"Wow, you're having a lucky day," the female employee gushed.

"You certainly are," giggled the older one on my left.

They went on.

"So, whatcha' think is going on? Just lucky?'"

"You're astrology sign kicking in? I'm a Taurus. What are you?"

"Are you psychic? My grandma was. She could tell when the phone was gonna ring. You like that? Can you tell which machine is gonna hit?"

Yada, yada, yada.

Their chatter distracted me. Which is exactly what it was supposed to do. I couldn't focus on playing. Plus, the fact I'm somewhat claustrophobic didn't help the situation. True, I was on a winning machine, but suddenly I started to lose. Five losing spins later, I cashed out and tossed more money into my purse and fled.

A cab carried me back to my hotel. It was only a matter of blocks, but I didn't trust myself to walk the strip with that amount of money. I'd either lose it to a mugger or give it back to another casino. As soon as I arrived at our hotel, I tipped the driver fifty bucks and jumped out of the cab and raced to my room.

Once inside, I spread the forty one-hundred-dollar bills across the bedspread. I sat back in an armchair, crossed my legs and waited for my husband to return. One thing for sure, that night we wouldn't be waiting in line for half price tickets to the cheapest show in town.

Day Three: Vegas

Vegas, baby ... senior style.

I headed to the shower, plugging in my hot pot along the way and limped into the stall. Fifteen minutes later I was sipping coffee so thick it could be eaten with a spoon.

Emptying the contents of my purse onto the bed, I began my daily ritual. Various coins had been lurking about in the bottom along with a few ticket-in, ticket-out slips I'd forgotten to cash. One was from Mandalay Bay for $1.23 and another from the Luxor for $2.52. Over the next few days there would be more tickets I'd forget about. On the last day, if I hadn't redeemed them, I'd leave them for the maid. In the past, the total of my unredeemed tickets came to twenty dollars or more. Not a bad tip, if you don't mind running around the city to claim it.

The coins in the bottom of my bag came to a total of $1.55. I slipped them into my little coin purse. I counted the bills from the zip side pocket that held my daily allowance. I undid the five different diaper pins that weaved through the zipper head and fabric on my bra wallet and removed the contents. I fanned the items out in front of me.

Driver's License: check
Primary credit card: check
Return ticket: check
Second ATM card: check.
Secondary credit card: check
Cash: check

Three blank checks: check
Social Security card: check
Card with meds and prescription: check
Health insurance card: check
Medicare Card: check
Phone card: check
Two four-day bus passes: check
Cash – count first, count again, and then: check

If I didn't do an inventory, I'd find myself panicking throughout the day. *Where's my fricking train ticket? How much money do I have left? Am I broke? Did I lose my credit card? Where's my ID?* I've stripped off almost all my clothing in a casino bathroom stall a few times to reassure myself I hadn't lost anything important.

A friend once said to me, "The way you have to travel sounds exhausting."

I answered, "It is."

Once I'd verified I had everything I needed to survive and return home, I checked it one more time before packing the items away in my bra wallet's various zipper compartments. The many diaper pins that held it all together were clicked shut. I tugged at each one just to make sure they were locked. I slipped on the bra wallet and didn't take it off again until the next morning, when I showered.

I even slept in the darn thing.

The last item on my agenda was to call housekeeping and request to not have service to my room during my stay. I'd rather reuse towels than have a stranger poke about where I sleep.

My cash had dwindled to a few dollars. It was time to hit the ATM.

If I withdrew cash every day for a week, I'd end up paying around fifty-six bucks in fees. If I'd ever applied for casino credit, I could, of course, cash a marker. But applying for a line of casino credit with the money due thirty days later, has never been an option for me. Neither is a credit card advance. The last thing I want is to have every credit card maxed out because I was convinced I was on "a roll".

If I do not have access to discretionary cash, I do not gamble. Period. The eight-dollar-a-day fee for using an ATM to access my own money is worth it.

I am a gambler, not an idiot. If I have to have an addiction, I'm glad it's based in sugar rather than playing the odds.

∞

Downtown Vegas is old, cheap and bordering on the indecent. I fit in perfectly.

Across the board prices for hotel rooms, restaurants, buffets and entertainment are far more reasonable Downtown than on The Strip. The slots are rumored to be looser while the minimum bids at the tables are definitely lower. The cover photo of this book of me winning a jackpot was taken Downtown.

I've had a few friends who detest Downtown because it is "sleazy". I like that it borders on the questionable. For a woman, I've always been "manly" in my disposition toward sex and nakedness. The more, the better. My good friend Pete loves our phone chats about life and love. He's always saying, "Talking to you is just like talking to a guy!"

And I respond, "Ah, thanks?"

My attitude can be traced to my discovering *Playboy* magazines at the vulnerable age of eleven. The stash wasn't hidden very well. I just had to open a dresser drawer and rummage around underneath my older brother's underwear.

After I discovered its existence, when my family headed out to church, I'd fake being sick in order to stay home. As soon as Dad drove down our gravel driveway, I'd spread out my wicked find on the green Formica kitchen tabletop. I'd read every article, study every sexist ad, and hold up each page with their titillating pictures sideways, upside down, and this way and that.

Sex in most American households in the '50s and '60s, was never discussed. Any information I acquired came from reading the pages of Huge Hefner in an era before the term sexism and chauvinist pig became the norm.

If I had been psychic, I would have waited a few years to develop my outlook on life. Gloria Steinem would have been my base of wisdom, not a greasy, geeky looking guy in a silk robe, smoking a ridiculous looking pipe and spouting a new world order based on sex first, a man's desires second, and everything else afterwards.

But a large part of my personality is the same as many of the men of my generation. When it comes to anything sexual, I turn into a kid who giggles at the sight of a jiggling butt (*She said butt!*). Or I laugh at innuendoes far too long to be anything but immature.

Downtown Vegas is one long adolescent sex joke without a punch line in sight. (*She's showing her boobies!*) You can't walk half a block without being confronted with sex, and then more sex. Especially when you're partaking in the Fremont Experience.

When someone mentions "Downtown", they're talking about a five-block-long pedestrian mall beginning on 4th and Fremont. The four blocks are shrouded by an overhead canopy of laser lights. Nightly, a spectacle of lights and images flash across the glass ceiling while music and sound effects blast in accompaniment.

Along the side streets of Fremont sits old school casinos like the El Cortez, California, or the Main Street. But Fremont Street itself is where most of the action lies and where the Deuce dropped me off at 11:00 a.m. on Saturday.

Behind me was the beginning of the Zip Line ride that travels high above the pedestrian mall. The Heart Attack Grill was behind me, offensive on so many levels to me. Patrons who weigh three hundred and fifty pounds can chow down, compliments of the house. As far as I could tell, the owners were making money off of a fat man's pain, yet presented it as a fun experience for all. Though I have been a comedian for a good part of my life, I couldn't just see the humor.

On the far corner, Denny's Restaurant bustled with guests. The travel forums I follow usually post questions from incoming British tourists asking if they need a reservation to dine at Denny's. The resounding answer is always a solid 'yes'.

Travel forums can be cruel.

Ahead of me, hundreds of tourists roamed the mall ending at the Plaza Hotel. By the end of the day, nearly twenty-five thousand people will have come and gone.

I crossed the street and passed by Crazy Ely Western Village, a combination of souvenir shop and off-sale liquor emporium. A gigantic yellow sign in the window proclaimed, "Alcohol purchased at this location CANNOT be consumed on the Fremont Street Experience." There is a continuing battle between liquor stores and bars. The current compromise is that all liquor consumed in pubic must be in a plastic container.

Within a half block I stumbled upon a site that made me vacillate between suppressing an urge to giggle while fighting the need to throw up. At a bit past eleven in the morning, the street was dotted with nearly naked street "entertainers." The image my eyes rested upon was not a pretty site.

Two pairs of sagging and unclothed buttocks were within a hand's reach. The butt cracks I unwillingly stared at were protected by a thin piece of fabric that disappeared somewhere between two hairy half-moons. The male duo proudly displayed their wares in vivid red mankinies, made famous by the actor Borat. On their balding heads were red cowboy hats, decorated with rhinestones and feathers. Scruffy brown cowboy boots completed their look. A plastic bucket rested in front of them with a hand printed sign taped to it, "Tips Appreciated!"

I scuttled past without contributing. To be fair, I appreciate a muscular tush or even a round, fleshy one. But, this set of drooping and crevice filled buns belonged to two men in their mid-60s whose faces looked like those plastered across anti-meth posters.

Tip-seeking costumed characters, celebrity lookalikes and scruffy panhandlers were beginning to fill the street. The licentious and ribald out-numbered the family safe entertainers two to one. Dora the Explorer stood next to four bare-breasted nuns with breasts the size of the Pope's hat, tiny pasties covering their nipples. The nuns were rigid and silent, repeatedly slapping a wooden ruler against their palms. Simply put, another photo-op in the making for the folks back home.

Continuing to stroll Fremont, I opted out of stopping by the Mermaid for a ninety-nine cent indulgence of either a deep-fried Oreo or deep-fried Twinkie. On a few of my visits, I've managed to consume both deadly treats. Instead, I slid into the Four Queens Casino to escape the street. The smell of cigarette smoke and noise made its assault. Electronic dings, bells, the sounds of fake and real coins hitting metal and a cacophony of chatter struggled to overcome the loud background R&B music.

For the most part, Downtown casinos are old school design with lower ceilings, narrow aisles, poor ventilation and god-ugly multi-colored carpeting. My plan was the same as always. Sit down at a machine and play until a smoker sat beside me. Then, unless I was on a winning streak, move quickly to another machine.

I'd hang around until nightfall, catch a bit of a free concert on the mall, and afterwards, head back to my hotel. Even at my age and with my limited mobility, I've never felt anything but safe being on Fremont Street.

Walking several aisles of the casino floor, I spied a Whale of Cash. I liked the game so much I'd downloaded the $1.99 app version on my computer.

Cheap, considering what I've paid to play it for real. I slipped in a twenty. Twenty-two games later, I finally scored a win of fifty cents. My gambling had barely started and I was already in the hole by ten dollars and fifty cents.

I lifted my butt up slightly to move when a bubbly woman and her friend sat down next to me. Slot players are usually somber, unless they're drinking or winning. These two gals held jumbo mimosas in their hands. Plastic cheese wedge earrings dangled from both sets of ears.

Cheeseheads! Wisconsinites on an early morning bender! I decided to hang around. I could use the entertainment.

One of the women's first spin landed her in the bonus round. The duo clinked their two plastic glasses hard. A mixture of champagne and orange juice sprayed over the top and on to the front of their Green Bay Packers sweatshirts.

"You go, Emma!" said her friend.

Emma ended up winning three hundred and seventy-eight dollars in the bonus round. Playing max play at five dollars a spin paid off for her.

"Good for you," I said, when the bonus ended and the dollar amount flashed on the screen.

Emma responded a friendly, "Thanks."

"Are you two from Wisconsin?" I asked.

The duo's loud laughter echoed over the singing of the slots. Emma's friend asked, "Gee, how can you tell?"

"I'm from Minnesota," I answered.

"Neighbor," Emma said before giving me a high five as a few splashes of her Mimosa jumped into my lap. She was too 'happy' to notice.

I sat with the two retired elementary school teachers for an hour, playing and snorting out laughs. We had a semi-serious discussion about Harry Potter and how boys who never read books ended up reading. A good story will do that.

We teased each other about which state was better, and who was better, the Vikings or the Packers. By the end of the hour, Emma was up five hundred and forty-two dollars and I was down a whopping two hundred and three.

My giggling stopped as soon as I came to my senses and realized what I'd lost. The machine wasn't about to pay me back my funds just because I was having a good time. I kicked myself in my virtual butt. If I wanted to taunt someone from a border state, I could usually do that in Minnesota for free. At the speed I was losing, I'd be out of cash by 2:00 p.m. and have to retreat back to Paris, just like Napoleon, my head hanging low in shame.

I bid the ladies adieu and shuffled back onto Fremont where the party atmosphere was beginning to take hold. The number of tourists and buskers had doubled. A mixed bag of professional entertainers, drunks dressed in tattered dirt encrusted costumes, teens banging on paint cans or break dancing lined the street. Overhead, the twelve-story slot themed Zip Line whizzed by me. The ride ended eight hundred and fifty feet from its launch pad.

As always, inside the entrance at the Golden Nugget, Big Bertha, a seven-foot tall and five foot wide giant slot, beckoned me. Like other tourists, I was mesmerized by its sheer size and sparkling colors of gold and glossy black. Just pulling down Big Bertha's giant lever would give my upper arm a workout.

Thirty seconds after entering the Golden Nugget, and leaving Bertha in my dust, I was down another ten bucks. *Crap!* There was only seventy-five bucks left to not only wager, but eat on for the rest of the day. Considering I was losing over a hundred bucks an hour, it was time to take a step back and focus on another addictive behavior. One that always gives me pleasure.

Eating.

The Garden Court buffet at the Main Street Casino and Hotel was two short blocks away. The brick structure, built in the '70s, features a Victorian theme accented with a piece of the Berlin Wall mounted in the men's room. Urinals are attached to the Berlin artifact. I have a feeling 'Take that, Russia' has been said more than once in the men's john.

The line for the buffet snaked forty feet, the wait to be seated ten minutes or so. I needed food and I needed it fast. Not that I was hungry, I wasn't. But nourishment is rarely a reason for me to eat. Anxiety was settling in. If I continued losing at the same speed, I'd be cash broke within an hour. The only thing that could stop the onslaught of incoming melancholia was a carb and sugar high.

The host asked, "How many?"

I answered, "One."

The same answer I'd cheerfully given since arriving in Vegas, now sounded sad. Feelings of loneliness were hanging around the edges of my consciousness, directly related to my financial status.

I've wondered often why I'm so attracted to something as stupid as playing slots, over and over, for days on end. After all, all I am doing is sitting there, poking with my finger until the tip actually hurts from overuse. At one time I made fun of folks who spent their nights in front of the boob tube, or did silly crafts all weekend long, such as decoupage.

Trust me on this one fact. There is *never* a reason for a coffee table to have thirty-four *Time* magazine covers varnished into its surface.

And there I was, not only spending my day poking away, but gleefully wasting away money that had taken an entire year to save.

The feelings of being a loser started to overwhelm me as I nibbled at salad greens and fruit slices. My snowball of depression started increasing in size. I knew if it didn't stop growing, I'd suffocate under an avalanche of bad feelings.

I rushed to the desert counter. Within seconds a bowl of sugar-free vanilla ice cream, ten strawberries dipped in sugar-free chocolate, and a dollop of sugar-free butterscotch pudding were sitting in front of me. I would still meet my calorie goal for the day, but it would all consist of chemical impersonators of sugar. By the end of the meal, I'd shoved my feeling of moroseness into the background, using ten pounds of granulated white powder as a wedge.

Outside the buffet doors, I decided to try my luck at Main Street. The meal had been good for me. Why not the gambling? I slipped a five into a Kitty Glitter machine. Back home in Minnesota I once won eight hundred and seven dollars on a dollar bet. I'd settle for a tenth of that at the moment.

Ten spins later, I headed toward the skywalk that connected Main Street with the California Hotel and Casino. Tallying my five-buck loss and lunch expense, I was down to sixty bucks. I might as well spend the rest of the afternoon watching the Hawaiians.

∞

The economic bubble and bust of the '90s had hit Hawaii the same as it did the Mainland. The islands' economy collapsed and inflation rose, big time. Tens of thousands of Hawaiians moved to Las Vegas seeking good jobs and cheaper housing. Currently over ninety thousand former Hawaiians call Vegas their home. Along with their migration, came their cuisine.

Spam Musubi is a popular snack, reminiscent of sushi featuring grilled Spam sitting on top of a block of white rice, the entire thing wrapped in dried seaweed called nori. The tasty and mile-high sodium laded treat is sold at convenience stores in Hawaii, and at The California in Las Vegas.

Another popular item is Loco Moco, white rice topped with a hamburger patty, fried egg and brown gravy. For a fast food junkie like me, nothing felt more like home than discovering Hawaiian cuisine that tasted like a special at a redneck diner.

Sam Boyd's California Hotel and Casino sits a block off Fremont and caters exclusively to the Hawaiian tourists. Built in the '70s, Boyd's alleged love of the islands convinced him to create a resort that not only celebrated the 50th state, but lured its residents away from paradise for their vacation. Forty years later, gambling junkets still arrive daily from the islands.

The Cal's clientele is largely Hawaiian and due to their food habits, they're larger than your average Joe. For the most part, the patrons are an older bunch. I fit right in as I shuttled past shops and restaurants with island motifs and beach murals.

I slid into a seat and within a few spins I was up twenty, then thirty. Woo hoo! A thirty-five dollar profit. Lady Luck was not only on my side, she was doing a hula dance. As long as I was on a roll, I might as well take a chance on winning my 'guaranteed' forty thousand dollars at roulette.

I've played roulette once or twice before. All I remember is that I walked away fairly quickly. It made me nervous. Being dyslexic, I couldn't trust reading the numbers in the grid board. But, according to the guy on the train, all I had to do was play the colors.

Stepping up to the table, my mind reran his instructions. Always play on the outside. Always choose to bet on red or black. Bet the same amount for two spins in a row, then cut in half on the next spin. After that, raise it to your original bet. "Rinse and repeat," he said, "until your pockets are stuffed with cash."

A bankroll of two hundred dollars was needed. Ninety-five bucks would have to do. It was all the money I had. Well, ninety if you counted the first bet I would place, which was nowhere near the guy's carefully thought out plans.

Four people already were at the table. The mood was jovial. The buxom croupier said, "Make your bets," right before giving the wheel a hard spin.

As the wheel clicked, five people placed bets on various numbers inside the grid, or on the outside bets like even, odd, red or black.

The croupier waved her hand across the table and announced, "No more bets."

The crowd waited as the little white ball bounced around the track inside the wheel. Finally, it landed.

"Number twenty-eight, even and red."

No one won, the happiness diminished slightly. But why would anyone win? Not a single player had chosen seventeen. That surprised me. That particular set of digits was the most played number in roulette. Experts believe it is the number one choice because it sits directly in the center of the grid. Others, like me, know the real reason. Seventeen was the number Bond, James Bond always played.

On instinct, I decided to toss the Amtracker's strategy aside, and bet on Bond's number. If I won straight up, the house would pay thirty-five times my five-dollar wager. A tidy one hundred seventy-five dollars. Three other players followed my lead.

The wheel spun round and then …

"Twenty-six, even and black."

Dammit....

Fifteen spins later, my ninety-five dollars had dwindled to twenty bucks. I walked away from the table cursing the Devil's Wheel.

∞

Four hours later, I was ready to flee Downtown. After my disastrous run at roulette, I'd cruised the casino floors looking for a ticket that might have been forgotten. I found one for thirty-three cents and another for a dollar and two cents. I slipped both into a machine. I won twenty cents, turned it into two dollars, and then lost the entire amount.

On the street, a busty mermaid-costumed cocktail waitress hung a cheap strand of green beads around my neck. Zipliners passed by overhead. I stood in a crowd and watched a Michael Jackson impersonator, two contortionists, and three close-up magicians. I released an "awww" when I saw an elderly couple dance slowly to a heavy metal rock n' roll band.

More almost-naked entertainers filled the streets. There was one set of boobs or buns after another. From obese to skinny, plain to beautiful, young to old, the debauchery began to get to me. I wanted to retreat to my hotel room, take a shower, and watch reruns of *The Brady Bunch*, or a *Dick Van Dyke Show*. Any programming that would prove life didn't have to be lived like it was lived on Fremont Street.

Twilight was setting in, and before the first laser show started, I was sitting on the Deuce bus heading back to The Paris. My loss for the day was $289.45. I could either beat myself up for losing, or pat myself on the back for having some cash left at the end of the day.

I opted for the *atta'girl.*

True, I had lost a substantial amount of money, but it was the exact amount of money I'd budgeted to lose. And there was still the chance I'd come out even, tomorrow.

My food was going well. Even with eating at Main Street Buffet, I'd managed to consume around twelve hundred calories. I'd stayed within the no sugar, no grain perimeters. Veggies, fruit, meat, fish and the occasional sugar-free, chemical laden, ice cream or pudding.

For dinner, I picked up a two-hundred calorie green salad again at the deli and carried it to my room. Though it was a Saturday night in Vegas, my old bones longed to be snuggled into a bed as I read about an adventure rather than live it.

Everything was perfectly fine and normal, until two hours later when I heard the lock on my hotel door jiggle.

101

∞

When I entered my hotel room earlier, the door seemed slightly ajar, as if it wasn't locked. The lock's light was green even before I slipped in my room key. I was able to push the door open with too much ease. Something was a bit off ... but then, so was I. Exhaustion was more than likely the reason for my heightened paranoia.

My eyes scanned the foyer and into the room. Clothes were strewn about on the floor, the beds, and the table. Brochures and newspapers were scattered on the floor. The table drawer was pulled open. Empty water bottles were scattered about on the counter, lying on their sides. The bedding was torn apart, the blanket, sheet and bedspread crumbled into a ball.

The room was exactly as I had left it.

If a burglar had been in my room, they hadn't taken a thing. I pushed the thought of a compromised lock to the back of my mind. Nothing was wrong. I was just tired and overly sensitive, like a toddler who'd missed their nap.

I ate my greens and a few strips of mozzarella cheese in peace. Afterwards, I slid an armchair in front of the door, knowing that act would certainly stop a potential break-in and delved into *Tracks* when the door rattled.

I bolted upright.

"Yes?"

A few more hard jiggles.

I swallowed hard. Someone was trying to break into my room. That explained the lock being tampered with earlier. I said in a very loud voice, with as much macho as I could muster, "Who is it?"

"Security," came back the muffled response.

"Security?" I asked, heading for the barricaded door.

Why I chose to head to the door, I could never understand. Not only was I naked, there was a weak barricade of an armchair standing between the door handle and me. Even if the chair wasn't there, I couldn't see out the peephole. Not only was I too short, but I'd done what every neurotic traveler does. I'd put duct tape over it.

I shouted back, "You're not security. I didn't call security."

The next sound I heard was, "Sorry, sorry. Wrong room."

I could hear someone shuffle away. My heart raced. I dashed to the phone and called the front desk.

"I think someone just tried to break into my room," I sputtered.

"What do you mean?" the woman asked in a not-so interested voice.

"Someone jiggled the lock. They said they were security. Did you guys send someone to my room?"

"I don't know," the woman answered honestly. I swear she was chewing gum. "I'll transfer you to security."

Ten minutes later, a guard stood in my room. He was polite as he gazed around the mess I'd made. "You said no one was in the room when you came back to it? And nothing had been trifled with or moved?"

I nodded and said weakly, "The lock seemed weird."

"Weird?"

"Like it wasn't locked."

"But it was locked?" he suggested.

I nodded.

The guard shrugged his shoulders, obviously not buying into my story. Casinos are used to dealing with false reports from hotel guests, all eventually claiming money was stolen, or jewelry taken in order to file an insurance claim. It was an all too common ploy designed to avoid admitting to the spouse back home where their money was actually lost ... on the gaming floor.

He said, "Okay, then. Let us know if anyone comes back."

"Wait, a minute," I insisted as he walked toward the door. "Can't you check the cameras? I write mysteries and …"

"Cameras?" he asked.

"Surveillance cameras. Don't casinos have video cameras all over the place."

He said nonchalantly, "Nah, we just have them in a few of the hallways." But then added proudly, "But they're all over the casino."

I wanted to answer, *Good! At least you know your slot machines are safe.*

Instead, I said firmly, "I don't want to stay here. There's no way I can sleep in this room."

"Call the front desk," he told me.

Over the phone, I was given an hour deadline to pack my bags and vacate. The hotel's key system is so automated and computerized the front desk was able to change the magnetic strip key card to work for my new room in Tower Two.

I hung up the phone and looked around the room. Crap. An hour seemed too short of a time. I'd have to somehow cram everything into my luggage, pack my sleep machine and meds carefully, without forgetting anything. An hour may seem like a long time, but not when you're old, obese and have to pick up half of your clothing from the floor. It took me forty-five minutes to finally leave the room.

By the time I reached the lobby, the casino was jam packed with revelers. Hoots and hollers were bouncing off the machines and card tables. Dings and electronic celebrations competed with loud drunks or just plain way too happy irritating people. Everyone seemed to have either a cigarette or a drink in hand, sometimes both. I maneuvered my way around thousands of people, pulling my luggage, while taking up more space than a human being is normally allowed.

Tower Two was on the other side of the gaming floor. My deluded mind, pictured a thirty-year old and way slimmer me, pulling my luggage and looking cute, sexy and available. In reality, I was a two hundred and twenty-five pound woman, huffing like she'd just run a marathon. Yet, I walked slower than a hundred-year old limping turtle with corns.

When I finally entered the room in Tower Two, I dead bolted it shut. It took me only a few minutes to duct tape the peephole, put two armchairs, the waste basket, the floor lamp, and the foldable luggage rack against the door.

Finally, I felt safe again. I was asleep within a matter of minutes.

Day Four: Vegas

Growing up in a fundamentalist Christian family in the '50s, Easter meant two things to me: a new dress for church and a candy-filled basket. I was more excited about the packaged goodies hidden behind green cellophane than the story of Jesus. Even as a young girl, I leaned toward the dark side, especially if it included chocolate.

When I woke up Easter morning in Las Vegas, a tinge of guilt hit me about not planning to attend church that day. That surprised me. I hadn't attended services on a regular basis in five decades. I'd long identified myself as the prodigal daughter who'd never bothered to return. Yet, Easter in Vegas had me haunted by the image of close-knit families worshipping together.

Perhaps I could just drop by a casino chapel to say "Hi there" to whatever gods might be hanging around? Hopefully, the chapels were open twenty-four seven. If not, they should have been. More urgently uttered and heartfelt prayers were raised in a casino than any place on earth.

All I knew was that I needed to get away from the strip. I was feeling the need for a calming environment. A place, as they say in Vegas hype, where "the locals go."

There were two free shuttle options to get off the strip. One shuttle carried riders to Sam's Town Hotel and Gambling Hall, a casino resort that catered to the working class. The other shuttle took gamblers to the far more elegant M Resort, located in the affluent

Southern Highlands neighborhood. Over coffee, I kept debating at which casino to spend my day.

My brother's face flashed before me. I remembered him telling me over and over how Sam's Town was one of his favorite places. It wasn't a question for me anymore. I'd head to Sam's.

For a change, I actually listened to what a family member had once told me.

Thank God, I did.

∞

I'll call him Mel.

The shuttle to Sam's Town originates in the covered parking lot behind Harrah's. Arriving fifteen minutes early, I waited on the hard plastic bench. An older woman sat down besides me and immediately buried her head in a tattered paperback. I strained to see the title. *The Fault in Our Stars*, a smattering of drama and sadness mixed in with triumph of spirit, appropriate for the ride.

A crowd began to form. A few would-be riders asked nervously if they had missed the 10:15 a.m. departure. I reassured them they hadn't. Gamblers and old people get antsy. Five minutes before the bus was scheduled to leave, it pulled into the parking space in front of me. A slew of passengers filed out. They were more than likely Sam's Town guests who would spend the day gambling on the strip.

The other casino, the one you are not playing at, is always the lucky one.

I stumbled up to be first in line. It's not that I thought I deserved priority seating. Instead, I love a driver who not only chatters but shares stories that only he would know. As usual, I will ask a gazillion questions, as if my true identity is Pat Dennis, Girl Reporter. I managed to grab the seat directly behind the driver.

Mel pulled out of the parking garage and maneuvered the large vehicle through the narrow road behind the casino. Eventually we were riding through Las Vegas neighborhoods of pawnshops, strip malls, fast food joints, and pay day loan establishments, each accented with swaying palm trees in front.

I started off the conversation with Mel. "How long have you been driving?"

"Seventeen years," he answered, slowing to a halt at a red light. "Started driving a shuttle bus the month after I moved to Vegas."

"Were you born here?"

"Nope."

"And you like driving a bus?"

"It's great," he answered. "Best job ever. I used to drive to the airport but for the last few years, I've been doing casino runs."

"It must be a lot of fun."

"It is," he answered. "Way better than the airport run. Folks are rarely happy when they leave Vegas."

I nodded in understanding. For a year of my life, I worked as a stand-up comic on tour buses going from Minneapolis to various casinos throughout Minnesota and Wisconsin. Thirty minutes before the tour bus would arrive at the casino, I'd perform a twenty-minute stand-up routine.

The bus gigs were some of the best I've had in my comedy career. Comedy is meant to be close and personal. And there's nothing more intimate than standing in a bus aisle, a cordless mic in your hand as you tell jokes from seat to seat.

I learned fairly quickly to only do my routine on the way to the casino, and never on the return trip. The chance of the captured audience being in a good mood on their way to a casino was a no-brainer. Coming back? Not so much. In fact, never. On the way back, I'd hide in the back seat, my face buried in a newspaper to avoid anyone asking for their tip back.

I decided to get serious with Mel, the Sam's Town driver. I asked. "Everyone talks about the winners. Got a special story about a loser?"

The older gentleman who sat across the aisle interrupted. I gathered he and Mel were former co-workers. The man retired from shuttle driving two years earlier.

"There was one lady I'll always remember," Bob said. "It was when I was driving an airport shuttle around ten years ago. I pulled up to the bus stop and loaded a dozen or so passengers. She just stood on the sidewalk, next to her luggage, looking dazed and hopeless."

Bob knew how to tell a story. He paused for dramatic effect. Eventually I asked, "What happened?"

He continued, "She told me she couldn't pay for the ride to the airport. She didn't have any money. I told her I couldn't let her ride for free. I'd get fired."

This time Mel said, "I know you, Bob. What did you do? You wouldn't leave her standing there on the corner."

"Nah, I wouldn't. The woman was older than me, for Pete's sake. I slipped her a five and told her to give it back to me on the bus. That way it'd look like she paid her own way. Surveillance camera," he explained.

"A surveillance camera on the bus?" I asked.

"Yep," he nodded.

So basically security cams are everywhere in Las Vegas except the hallway outside my hotel room. Gheesh!

Bob continued, "On the ride to the airport, she said she was a retired nurse. It was her first visit to Las Vegas. First time she ever gambled."

Mel said, "That's not good."

"It wasn't. She played craps, badly. Within two weeks, she maxed out all of her credit cards, and managed to empty out her savings account of forty-four grand. All she had left was a plane ticket home."

"Wow," I said, realizing there, but for having an actual career with a pension fund, go I.

Bob said, "I heard from her six months later."

"Really?" I asked.

"She'd asked for my name and address. She promised to pay me back the five bucks."

"Did she?"

"She mailed me a check for fifty bucks. I didn't cash it. Vegas had taken advantage of her. I didn't want to do the same."

∞

I like Sam's Town Hotel and Gambling Hall. The architecture is playful with a wild-west theme. Designed to resemble an old time western town, it managed to include an eighteen-screen cinema and a fifty-six-lane bowling alley as part of its allure.

Sam's promotes itself as a place locals like to go, the implication being Vegas residents have an inside scoop on gambling. I prefer to think it's because the locals, who are often employed in the tourist industry, frankly get tired of tourists. I know I would. One too many angry and disappointed Real Housewives of New Jersey gamblers would drive me over the edge fairly quickly.

The gamblers on Easter were sparse. I'd been at Sam's before and the place was always hopping. It was a religious holiday. Perhaps the townies were attending church, just like my mom always said I should do.

A sting of latent fundamentalist dread hit me. I'd totally forgotten about my decision to visit the chapel at the Excalibur. Now, it was too late. I was checked out of the Ex and my luggage was waiting to be claimed later at The Paris bellhop station.

I roamed around for a few minutes and ended up at the twenty-five thousand square foot open-air atrium named Mystic Falls. Sam's Town's indoor park contained tall living trees, babbling brooks, animatronic woodland animals and chirping birds. A river flowed through the park and ended at a gigantic rippling waterfall. Directly in front of the waterfall, a wedding was taking place.

When I saw a wedding officiate holding a bible in his hands, I smiled. I had ended up at a church service after all.

A small group of family members were gathered, watching the ceremony. The young bride and her beau held hands and listened to the minister talk about not entering the marriage lightly, but reverently.

The bride wore a white satin, strapless ball gown. Her waistline was encrusted with red and silver beading. Her three bridesmaids wore the exact same gown but in red satin while the beading at the waistline was white and silver. The groom and his men were sharp in their black tuxedos and red cummerbunds. But it was the ring bearer that made me tear up.

The boy reminded me of my nephew, fifty-some years earlier. He was the typical four-year old who thrived on mischief. If the young boy could do what he wanted to do at the moment, it would be running around the park at full-speed or climbing its trees to the highest limbs. It was obvious he'd only agreed to do the wedding gig if he could do it his way. Over the four-year old's tiny tuxedo was his red Superman cape.

The moment the groom kissed the bride, the crowd broke into applause and I headed to the gaming floor. Seeing a family wedding was a pleasant way to start the day. Watching a ceremony filled with hope for the future made me happy.

I was about to get a whole lot happier.

Buffalo Stampede is one of my favorite games to play. Although it is a "penny machine" the minimum bet is seventy-five cents. Still, if the wheels line up just right, the payoff can be enormous. I decided to slip in two twenties and let the fun begin.

In the early '80s, thousands of my quarters were lost to playing Pac Man. On one comedy trip in North Dakota, two comedians forcibly stopped me from playing a crane claw machine. Before they'd arrived,

I'd lost a hundred bucks trying to win a three-dollar stuffed animal.

Buffalo Stampede has that same draw for me. Not only does a herd of buffalo charge at the player at certain times during the game, there are bonuses with chances to retrigger automatically. Back on the plains, I've won as many as eighty-five games in a bonus, and as much as five hundred dollars.

The design consists of four-wheels and five columns of images including wolves, antelopes, cougars, and more. The audio is a mixture of eagles screeching or the sound of a buffalo herd stampeding. In the bonus round, all of the wild symbols pay two times, three times or four times the amount on the machine, and makes a major difference in the win amount.

I was down to the last dollar from my initial forty, when I hit the bonus round. Eight free games! I retriggered immediately when two gold coins appeared. After that, the retriggers kept coming. And so did the wins. By the time of the last bonus spin, I was up $654.50.

I rushed to the cashier and traded in my ticket for cash. Six hundred dollar bills ended up in the zippered compartment of my purse. Once I could breathe fairly normally again, I hunted down the Firelight Buffet. It was time to eat.

∞

Easter Sunday's Champagne Brunch, including the bubbly, was only $13.99. But the low price didn't really matter. I still had two hundred sixty dollars in cash left from my daily ATM withdrawal. Plus, the six hundred dollar jackpot from the Buffalo Stampede was barricaded in my wallet behind zippers and firmly clasped diaper pins. Deducting the cost and a five-dollar tip to the server, I had close to nine hundred dollars.

Not only was I rich, but I was on a *bona fide* winning streak. Maybe I'd even break my four thousand dollar record by the end of the day.

It could happen!

The line for the Firelight Buffet was surprisingly short. Within a few minutes I was grabbing a slab of Easter ham and slamming it onto my plate. I added a mountain of Brussels sprouts, green beans *almondine,* and fresh organic greens with olive oil and vinegar drizzled on top. Even with the egg white veggie omelet I planned on eating in my second round of food consumption, I'd still be within my calorie count for the day.

The table I sat at provided stuffed bench seating on one side and a chair on the other. It provided a perfect view of the milling crowds around the food stations. The clientele were either senior citizens or young families, taking advantage of a holiday feast for so little cost. A few of the tiniest girls wore Easter bonnets.

The number of single eaters equaled the parties of two or more. Las Vegas is a town where you can eat alone, and not feel like an odd duck. Though, not for a second, was that a guarantee for not feeling lonely.

"Having a good day?" I asked the woman seated a few feet away from me on the stuffed seating.

"Not really," she muttered in repressed fury.

I didn't know whether to pursue the conversation or not. There were times when my depression was stopped in its tracks by a mere hello from a stranger. Other times, a hint of a friendly salutation would send me deeper into despair.

"It's bound to get better," I told her cheerfully. "It's a holiday."

"I hate holidays," she answered.

I couldn't help but laugh loudly. I answered, "To be totally honest, I do too."

And with that we two old curmudgeonesses bonded and chatted gleefully about life's

113

disappointments and how we'd each soon have our foot in the grave.

And not a moment too soon! She said with a chuckle.

It turned out to be a good casino lunch, after all.

My manically good mood was still in full rev when I returned to gaming. I never played max bets or dollar machines unless I played with 'their money'. But I was in the black, and feeling fine. Besides, if I gambled more than usual, it wasn't a big deal. After all it was their money I was playing with, not mine.

No one was seated at either of the Megabucks progressive dollar machines. That surprised me. Gamblers were very superstitious and often believed that lightning would strike twice. Only three weeks earlier seventy-eight-year old Trinidad Torres won $10.7 million at the Westgate on a Megabucks progressive.

The story was all over the web. Headlines were somewhat brutal, in my opinion. One site blasted across its webpage, *Elderly Utah Woman hits $10.7 million jackpot in Las Vegas*.

But then, with the amount of money at stake, I don't know if I'd actually be bothered by my potential headline: *Fat Old Woman in Las Vegas wins millions.*

A few million would certainly help to heal an injured age-conscious ego.

Five twenties were fed into the slot. If I was going to go for the big one, I might as well start big. I hit max play and watched the wheel spin. When it finally stopped, nothing. Not a dime.

Like a good solider, I continued to battle. I'd win a little and then lose a lot. It took me a little more than ten minutes to see zero credits registered on the machine. I was about to leave in a huff when a woman sat down beside me to play. My competitive nature took hold. What if she won the moment I walked away? I'd be ticked off at myself for giving up.

One hundred and sixty dollars, the rest of my day's allowance, waited in my side pocket. I didn't have to

114

undo a single diaper pin to access it. The real money stash—the six hundred dollars—was safely hidden away.

I slid the entire one hundred and sixty dollars in the machine and hit max again. Within a half hour I was swearing nonstop as I headed outdoors. I'd lost every cent of my daily allowance.

The shuttle bus back to the strip was scheduled to arrive in twenty minutes. I plopped my body on a concrete bench and spent a few minutes chastising myself for chastising myself. I was still way ahead for the day. There were still six big ones in my possession. There was no reason to feel guilty. It's not like I spent every dime I had on me.

Suddenly, I realized I didn't have any money in my pocket to tip the shuttle driver. Though it wasn't a requirement, I refuse to ride in a shuttle bus, van, or taxi, or eat in a restaurant unless I can tip. I worked too long and too hard in the service industry in my twenties and thirties not to leave a gratuity.

Ten minutes later, I removed the first of the one hundred dollar bills hidden away. It took me only a few hours more to lose five hundred and eighty-five dollars. I had only fifteen bucks left when I finally boarded the shuttle van in defeat. I tipped the driver three dollars and clung onto my last twelve. I still needed to tip the bellman at the Paris and find some sort of cheap, healthy dinner. I was completely out of cash until the next morning when I could access the ATM machine.

What would have happened if I'd chosen to spend the day at the M resort? I wondered over and over, berating myself for making what I thought was a bad decision.

I found out when I turned on a local television station hours later.

∞

Paris Hotel

By the time I checked into the Paris hotel, the sky was black and the streets were lined with a river of lights. Outside the front doors, a massive glass and neon replica of a hot air balloon with the single word Paris written in lighted cursive script served as the hotel's marquee. Next to it, a brightly lit, five hundred -forty-one-foot-tall Eiffel Tower doppelganger shone like a welcoming beacon.

I'd settled comfortably into my room at the Paris. The décor was a bold salute to all things French. Deep blue carpeting, striped wallpapered walls, rich fabrics and dark wood comforted me after the day's loss. I nibbled away at a salad and clicked on the television. The breaking news caused my heart to skip a beat. My eyes rolled immediately upward and thanked whatever God was watching over me. I'd made the right decision after all on where I spent my day, even if I'd lost all my money at Sam's Town.

A man had shot himself in the head at the buffet line at the M Resort. According to the newscaster, the buffet was packed at the time. As soon as the shots rang out, confusion and panic spread. Customers ducked under tables or ran out of the buffet screaming. A few just sat in sheer, frozen panic.

The event had happened a few hours earlier. I opened my iPad and searched the Internet. It was still too early for a complete story but I knew there would be people posting on the web, already filling in the details, correctly or not.

The victim was fifty-three-year old John Noble, a man who'd sent a two hundred and seventy-page manifesto to a local news outlet, as well as a DVD voicing his frustrations at the M Resort. He'd also posted YouTube videos.

Five years earlier, Noble won an Eat - for - Free - for - Life Pass at the Studio B Buffet at the M Resort. Two years later it was revoked by the M. According to the reports, Noble supposedly had been banned for harassing female employees.

He tried to pursue legal action, but couldn't afford a lawyer. Not one single attorney in Las Vegas would take it on as a pro bono case. Eventually, Noble's depression and rage got to him. He claimed he wanted the world to know what he'd suffered. And he did just that on Easter Sunday, a day when the M was filled with guests and families.

The story disturbed me deeply. I understand depression all too well. I've suffered from it since I was a child. I remember being in fourth grade, sitting alone on a playground, wishing I were dead. Or more to the fact, that I'd never been born. I've fought the battle of dark moods and debilitating depression all of my life. As a young girl I felt my spirit shatter when my mother told me "being crazy" ran in my family. I knew she was talking about me.

For the rest of the evening in The Paris, I sat alone, staring out the hotel window. The faux Eiffel Tower was in my view as well as a million flashing lights from the rest of the city. The Las Vegas suicide rate was one of the highest in the nation. Much of it, I assumed was gambling related.

Taking one's own life over lost wages and dreams does not just happen in the desert. A cop friend once told me the roads in front of casinos across the nation are lined with suicides. They are never reported by the news outlets out of "respect" for the victim. Not to mention the effect on a casino's revenue if they were reported.

Suicide happens for many reasons. Even those with a rosy financial future and not an addiction in sight, take their own lives. But still, I had to wonder why I was so attracted to competing in a world where taking one's own life was often the end result.

Day Five: Vegas

The chirping of annoyingly loud fake crickets stirred me out of my slumber, reminding me one more time to change my friggin' ringtone. "Hello," I mumbled. It was 6:08 a.m.

"You still sleeping? I figured you'd be up," my husband said, no hint of an apology in sight.

"Time difference," I answered, rubbing my eyes.

"You see the news this morning?"

"Ah, you just woke me up," I reminded him.

"There was a suicide at the M yesterday. A man blew his head off in the buffet line."

"Well, I don't think it was blown off, but yeah, I saw the report. Sad. Where did you see it?"

"TV, on the Daily Mail web site. It's all over the news."

"Really?" I responded before changing the subject. I'd already put too much energy into thinking about John Noble's demise. "What are you up to today?"

Our conversation lasted twenty minutes or so. Only after hanging up did I began my morning ritual of sipping coffee, doing a bra-wallet inventory, and writing in my journal.

I'd made two vows before leaving on my trip. One, to my Facebook followers that I would be making a series of short videos of me wagering twenty bucks in every casino on the strip; I'd given up on that vow on

Day Three. Being an overnight YouTube star was not in my future; nor was the ability to figure out how my iPod camera worked.

The second pledge was made to my online, private writer's group. I'd committed to writing a minimum of 500 words every day on my trip. My scribbling's goal was to eventually transform my words into a travel memoir. I'd already come up with a possible title—*Fat Old Woman in Las Vegas ... Gambling, Dieting, and Wicked Fun.*

It was the *wicked fun* part that was giving me trouble.

At sixty-six years of age, being wicked was decades behind me. I didn't drink anymore. Nor did I inhale drugs, pick up men, or flirt with snotty, conservative right-wing women just to irritate them. Yet, if I wanted to include the word wicked in my title, I had to come up with something I could do easily and would not get me arrested. However, getting busted would increase book sales, especially if I ended up on COPS.

I wondered what wickedness I could find as I prepared to leave my room before catching my reflection in a mirror. Even with my Raquel Welch wig and zebra-striped top, I still looked like Wilford Brimley in drag.

It would be easier to remove the word wicked from the title.

Unless, I ... well, yeah...I could do that.

∞

Mon Ami Gabi, a French bistro in the Paris casino extends to an outdoor seating area on Las Vegas Boulevard. Situated directly across the street from the Bellagio fountains, the view is spectacular. The patio was filled with patrons sitting under outdoor heating lamps as they ate blueberry crepes or fluffy omelets. For my thickened Minnesota blood, the early morning, mid-fifty-degree temperature felt like a sauna. In

119

Nevada, the furnaces are turned on when it falls below sixty degrees. Two people walked by me wearing down jackets. The duo undoubtedly were locals who'd moved to Vegas for one-hundred degree-plus weather.

An RTC bus stop is in front of the Paris. At a little after 9:00 a.m. three-dozen people waited to board the bus when it arrived. Because of the number of riders getting off and on, and the time it takes for that to happen, it was often quicker to walk the strip.

After seeing no bus in site, I decided to do just that. Or at least give it a try. If it took three hours to walk what I used to do in one, so what? I had the time. There would be plenty of rest stops along the way.

My itinerary for the day was to eventually end up at the north end of The Strip at the newly opened SLS casino, formerly known as the Sahara. It was there I planned to do my dirty deed to achieve a bit of wickedness status. Or at least I would be wicked in my ultra-conservative dead mom's eyes.

But first, I needed to start moving.

The sidewalks were dotted with tourists and hucksters. Costumed street entertainers lined the streets, tip buckets placed in front of them. Two Elvis impersonators in white bellbottom jumpsuits with red pleated slits on the side waited patiently to earn their keep. Red scarves hung around their necks and drifted down their potbellied fronts. Wide rhinestone belts circled their waists. Sparkly embellishments of various colors dotted their sleeves and formed an image of an American Eagle on their backs. All in all, it looked like a BeDazzler had thrown up on the two.

Between the two Elvis impersonators stood a living "Welcome to Las Vegas" sign. The iconic costume covered a much shorter individual whose face and torso was hidden under the fabric sign. His eyes peeked out through tiny slits at the top of the sign. The Elvis pair rested their hands on the top of the faux sign as they waited for pictures to be taken for photo hungry tourists.

A few feet beyond, I came upon my first physical challenge of the day. The escalator leading to the pedestrian bridge spanning Flamingo Avenue was broken. Pedestrians were forced to walk up the packed stairway located between the up and down escalator. Foot traffic was not allowed to cross the busy avenue by foot.

I had two choices, to struggle up the steep concrete steps to the bridge, an estimated forty or so steps, or find the elevator provided for the physically disabled.

Walking up the steps to the bridge was not an option for me. I wasn't lazy. Climbing any steps was a daunting and exhausting experience. I'd place one foot on a step and stop. Then I would bring my other foot to the same level and stop again. Then I'd repeat the process over and over again until I made it to the top. In Las Vegas there were too many antsy and rude people to attempt my painfully halting version of stair climbing.

I discovered the lift directly behind the staircase. When the elevator doors shifted opened I muttered, "Shit!"

Lying on the metal floor inside was a man, passed out drunk. His clothes were filthy and torn, his long grey hair matted. An empty pint bottle was still clasped firmly in his hand. The entire cubicle smelled like stale whiskey and fresh urine.

I stood there motionless, afraid to enter the space alone. Luckily, a young couple rushed up to catch a ride. Their reaction to the unfortunate being was to laugh, rather than cringe in horror. The lovebirds stepped inside and I stepped in front of them.

The scene was only a bit more cheerful when I exited the lift. A trio of homeless people were scattered along the bridge, holding up various signs made from cardboard boxes. The slogans ran from "Hungry. Need food. God Bless," to "Ain't gonna lie. Need Dope." Before the day's end I would see dozens of beggars, many of them pathetically real, many of them obnoxiously bogus.

In the middle of the overpass, a man stood over a large cooler of bottled water.

"One dollar each," he barked in a heavy Mexican accent.

I handed him two bucks and took one bottle.

"*Gracious*," he said with a smile.

"*De nada*," I responded, and rode the escalator to the street.

I passed the small boutique hotel and casino, The Cromwell. Under a new name, the renovated resort had only opened a year earlier. Before, when it was Bill's Gambling Hall and Saloon, I stopped by on every trip. My favorite free-to-see entertainer was a featured performer called Big Elvis, aka Pete Vallee. He had the kind of body and voice that filled a room. At one point in his life, he weighed nine hundred pounds. He'd slimmed down to a more reasonable five hundred within the past few years.

Pete was an incredible singer, but his ability to interact with an audience was where his true charm lied. When The Cromwell decided not to include him in their new entertainment line-up, they made a mistake. For many tourists, including myself, there was no reason to drop by The Cromwell. Elvis had left the building.

Instead, I headed to the Flamingo.

Two years before I was born, and after a complete renovation, Bugsy Siegel opened the Flamingo. The first night's star-studded gala included Clark Cable, Judy Garland, Joan Crawford and Lana Turner.

Today the headliners are Donny and Marie.

Oh, well.

I squirrelled my way down the sidewalk, passing street vendors and beggars. A light breeze caused the top of the palm trees lining the sidewalks to wave as traffic whizzed by on The Strip.

Ding-ding-ding-ding-ding-ding-ding sounds assaulted my ears as soon as I entered the Flamingo. Following the audible trail, I was soon standing behind a woman at a Blazing Sevens dollar slot machine. A thousand-dollar jackpot flashed on the screen.

"Congratulations," I said. Her grin was wide. Her enthusiasm to the edge of hyperventilation. A newbie, obviously. She was way too excited, even for winning a grand. An experienced player would know a thousand dollars usually turns into two thousand lost.

She pointed across the aisle to a similar machine. "A woman hit the same thing last night right over there. These machines are great!"

The hopes of catching her good karma by playing close to her was tempting. I resisted however, not quite ready to begin losing my money. I worked my way through the maze of bright lights, sirens, and mid-morning chatter, and watched as other people lost theirs.

A small group of lanyard wearing conventioneers, men and women, gathered around Kate. I know her name because they kept repeating it in cheer-like fashion.

"Kate! Kate! Kate!"

Grimacing, she pressed the button on a five-dollar machine. With every spin of the wheel, her compatriots' cheers grew louder. When the reel stopped and three bars or three sevens did not appear, a loud groan emitted the group. Then, within seconds the crowd would start to chant her name again.

I continued past and stopped in front of Bugsy's Cabaret. Six larger-than-life images of scantily dressed women stared down at me from the walls. I paused, not to stare, but to wonder if seeing the show would qualify as my being wicked, especially if I saw it alone. How many sixty-six-year old women were in the audience lusting after a dozen female boobs?

Who was I kidding? It was 2015. Hundreds, especially if they found a half-off coupon.

I continued toward the Flamingo's wildlife habitat. I longed to see real Flamingos, the kind Alice used as croquet mallets. I exited through the glass doors and walked a winding path, past streams and minuscule waterfalls. Turtles, ducks, swans and parrots moved about. After being in Vegas for only five days, I ached to touch nature, even if it came with showgirls as a backdrop. The ringing of my phone had me spying a bench. I slowly hurried toward it.

"Good morning," I said, sitting down. My husband couldn't have chosen a better time to call. I would actually be telling the truth when I announced I wasn't in a casino.

"Where are you?" he asked.

I proudly answered, "At the gardens at the Flamingo Hotel."

"Oh yeah?" he answered, not sounding totally convinced. "Why?"

"I needed someplace to sit and think. I want to do something wicked today. I can't figure out what."

"Oh yeah," he mumbled back again in response. "So, I'm thinking about painting the back porch and …"

My husband never listens to a word I say.

Or perhaps he realized my doing something wicked with my body would mean I'd have to invent time travel first and then travel backwards by three decades.

Steve and I chatted for twenty minutes or so. By the time I left the gardens, it was past 11:00 a.m. and I'd yet to wager. Impressed with my discipline, I promptly plopped down at a machine and lost ninety bucks.

∞

I pondered.

I ponder a lot when I gamble, especially if I lose. Winning doesn't provide me the opportunity to review my life and its tsunami of bad choices. Nor does coming out ahead set me off on a spiritual quest for salvation or an explanation of the pollution in my life.

Nope.

If I win? I sit grinning like an idiot.

124

Ah, but losing!

I sat there stirring my tea, satiated from a feast of greens, fruits, cold shrimp, grilled salmon, mounds of sugar-free pudding, and cheesecake sans the graham cracker crumb crust. Cravings at the Mirage was a buffet I visited every trip. My husband and I have stayed at the resort a dozen or more times. The buffet feels like home, if my dining room were thirty-two thousand square feet with ten different international food stations scattered around it.

Mid-afternoon found me tired, but I refused to go back to my room, retreating in shame because my vacation was still G-rated. I found comfort in losing another sixty-two dollars at the nearest slot. Including the cost of lunch, I was down one hundred and eighty-one dollars for the day.

The tram between the Mirage and Treasure Island took longer than if I'd chosen to walk the distance. But it allowed for sitting, something I need to do, a lot. When I made it to Treasure Island, I walked directly through the gaming floor, stopping only to smell the Krispy Kreme store in the hallway. It was 4:00 p.m. by the time I walked over the pedestrian bridge and ended up at the Fashion Show across from the Wynn.

My final destination was to be at a particular shop at the SLS casino, a mile and a half north on The Strip. It had taken me over six hours to reach the midway point of my journey. I debated on retreating into the food court at the mall for a respite. The only other option I considered won out.

I decided to gamble across the street at the Wynn for "only a few minutes" before continuing my quest for debauchery. Besides, I needed to say hello to my second favorite S man, casino mogul Steve Wynn.

I didn't expect to see the man himself. But his image was plastered across both the property and the casino's Megabucks slot machines. Nowhere else have I seen the owner of a casino's image pop up on a game monitor, speaking to you as if you were his best friend.

Steve Wynn produces a strong reaction from the public and the press. He seems to be either loved or hated. I admired him for one reason. He banned Terrance Watanbe from gambling at his casinos.

∞

One of the biggest whales to flop around the gaming floors in Vegas was a novelty salesman from Omaha, Nebraska. Terrance Watanabe lost more than two hundred million dollars playing blackjack and twenty-five-dollar multi-line slot machines, badly. According to a few casino employees, Watanabe was laughingly bad in his skill set.

His ability at handling his liquor was no better and, according to Watanabe and his attorneys, Caesars and the Rio casinos supplied him with alcohol and pain killers to facilitate his gambling addiction.

But not Steve Wynn.

After Watanabe lost twenty-one million at The Wynn, he was called into Steve's office to have a 'chat'. Wynn told Watanabe he was a compulsive gambler and a drinker and that he was no longer welcomed at the Wynn properties. Nor was his money.

I still find myself shaking my head at Watanabe sometimes. Not that he had gambled away his family's wealth. That happens. Period. Whether the family is worth twelve bucks or twelve million, when a compulsive gambler starts gambling, there is rarely a happy ending.

But what rattles me is the story behind the story. The family business that Watanabe owned, The Oriental Trading Company, made over three hundred million in sales a year selling plastic trinkets and gag gifts to the carnival market. A year! And that's for merely importing a cargo shipload of whoopee cushions.

I've spent my life writing and have earned a piddling amount of money. If I had been wiser, my time would have been better spent selling stuffed animals that farted.

∞

I finally arrived at the SLS, formerly known as the Sahara, the iconic Rat Pack's hangout. It was located at the far north end of the strip, in an area often referred to as a wasteland because of the abandoned hotel projects, cheap motels and numerous tattoo parlors and pawn shops. Under new ownership, and a four hundred and fifteen million dollar makeover by famed designer and architect Phillipe Starck, the SLS was the must-see property in town.

The real reason I had wanted to visit SLS was a recently opened, small "hidden sex" shop inside the property. A few of the posters on trip forums had written descriptions of the shop's inventory. Naughty lingerie, leather attire and accessories, and a multitude of sex toys.

However, the online chat that caught my eye concerned a certain piece of inventory on display that caught my attention—a special edition of a golden vibrator shaped like Queen Elizabeth.

When I came to my senses and decided not to waste any of my precious time on checking out a royal sex toy, I wondered if I was actually somewhat of a hypocrite. Call me a prude, but Queen Elizabeth just doesn't do it for me.

So instead, I found myself waiting for the bus, my virtue still intact, when I saw a short, chubby man standing nearby, handing out handbills to anyone who'd take them. The man provided me an answer. I could still be wicked, after all. I eagerly approached him, holding out my hands like a demented Oliver Twist.

127

His uniform was a pair of worn jeans and an orange t-shirt with white lettering blazoned across the front, "Girls Direct To You in Twenty Minutes." For convenience, a phone number was written in smaller letters underneath the promise of service to your hotel room within a matter of minutes.

Called 'porn slappers', the huskers are men or women who distribute handbills, the size of a postcard, for erotic services available throughout the city. Though the images on the cards are not pornographic, they certainly are erotic, if not downright filthy. Women of all ages are pictured naked with only stars or strips covering their naughty bits while their poses suggest they earned a master's degree in contortionism.

Handing me a card, the gentle Hispanic man asked, "Lesbian?"

"Minnesotan," I answered.

I took a gander and held up three more fingers. He looked embarrassed as he slipped me a small stack, perhaps a dozen in all. Poor guy. More than likely, he was a conservative family man just trying to earn a few extra bucks to feed his kids.

Walking back to the bus stop I clutched my proof of decadence. My book title was justified. I wouldn't actually call the numbers on any of the cards. Just the fact that I didn't tear them up in a feminist rage against the depravity of man, proved so sleazy that a few of the bus riders stepped back when they saw what I held in my hands.

A few of my conservative friends would call it sinful. I felt good. Elated, actually. So much so, I was caught off guard when, on the very next day, as I pleaded for my life, I decided it might be a good idea to abandoned vulgarity and focus on redemption.

At least until I was safe and not waiting to be killed.

Day Six: Vegas

The day I became the town fool started as a typical vacation day. Groggy after a fitful night's sleep, I stumbled to the windows and yanked the royal blue curtains open. The Vegas skyline and half-sized Eiffel Tower was directly in my view. The sky was vast and clear. Below me, the waters of the Paris's pool shimmered in the morning sun. The lush landscaping dotted with greenery and marble statues provided the illusion of a Parisian garden.

It was too early for sun-worshippers to be out, but lounge chairs were already placed around the octagon shaped concrete natatorium, private cabanas available for rent if you could afford it. Their prices, depending upon the season, ranged from the lower hundreds to one thousand dollars for the day. They were a not-so-gentle reminder that I would always be a peasant. There were people out there in the world with a staggering amount of money, a wealth I could not even begin to comprehend.

My daily penance, which oddly enough wasn't associated with gambling, began with opening my laptop. For fifty some years writing had turned into a punishment rather than a joy — a direct result of all the "shoulds" that I shat upon my craft.

I should write that novel. I should write a thousand words a day. I know I should make as much money as

129

James Patterson and treat my family members to a Mercedes. I should ...

The creative process did give me joy, but only when my bruised ego and spirit stepped aside to let it flow. I zone out when I step into writing, just like I do when I gamble. When the writing is going well time whizzes by. When it is going badly I trudge through a river of muddy words wearing knee high waders and clichéd metaphors.

While traveling, being a member in an online writers' group keeps me on track. After I made the daily word count, I'd report every morning to my peers. I'd post "did my five hundred words, time to hit The Strip." I'd receive back a round of "Atta girl!" or "Win a fortune!"

On day six, as soon as I finished my demiurgic gesture and hit "save", my telephone rang.

"Hey there," I said, not even bothering to look at the caller ID. No one else calls me on my pre-paid flip phone.

"Tomorrow, eh?" my husband asked. He was referring to the start of my two-and-a-half-day trek home. My husband was either missing me or sadly counting down his hours of freedom left.

"Yeah," I answered. "It's gone by quick."

It always does.

"You can stay longer if you want to," he informed me.

"Right," I say, somewhat sarcastically.

If I did stay, we'd be homeless in a matter of months. I can stick to a budget of three hundred dollars a day for seven days. Not too financially devastating since I'd taken a year to save the money to squander. But, I'd spend the same amount daily in Vegas if I were there for one day, a month or a year. Once I find a comfort point, no matter how uncomfortable it becomes, I always return to it.

"What are you doing today?" he asked.

"I have a fifty percent off coupon for the Monte Carlo buffet. Then I'll probably gamble at City Center, and afterwards take the bus to Circus Circus."

"Going to get some exercise sometime today?"

He always asked that question.

"Sure."

I always lied with my answer.

After we said our goodbyes, I scrambled to find the television remote. It was somewhere under the pile of clothes scattered about on the floor, bed and tabletop. Ten minutes later, I restrained from throwing it at the TV.

Though it was April, snow was still piled high in my yard at home. The Vegas TV weatherman warned, in all the seriousness someone with a degree in meteorology from a community college could muster, a low front was coming in the next day. It would be one-degree below normal. The high, a mere seventy-one degrees.

Within a half-hour, dressed in a flowing cheetah tunic top, brown Capri leggings and dangling zebra earrings, I waited in line at the ATM. Another three hundred dollars would be withdrawn from my account, and if things kept going the same way, it would vanish by the end of the day. Still, there was always a chance that a single jackpot would eliminate any loss on the trip.

Hope and stupidity spring eternal.

At least with wagering, optimism was something I'd yet to discard. I'd pretty much given up on any other lifelong dream materializing. As hokey as it sounded, only by losing was there any chance for me to become a winner.

∞

On the sidewalk, I performed my annual curse-a-thon at the labyrinth known as the entrance to Planet

Hollywood. The sidewalk disappeared in front of the casino. Instead, I had no choice but to climb steep concrete steps to the landing in front of the casino doors. The elevated walkway was out of order, and this time no elevator was provided for the handicapped.

I decided to cross the street and take the free City Center tram to the Monte Carlo instead. To do that, I had to cross the street and head to the back of the Bellagio. Distance wise, it would be the same. But my feet would enjoy taking a breather from being slammed repeatedly into a concrete sidewalk. Plus, I'd get to take in the impeccable ostentatiousness and beauty that is the Bellagio.

There is nothing subtle about the B. It is all glitz, glam and gaudiness starting with the exterior's eight-acre man-made lake with lighted, dancing fountains. Inside, the ceilings are high, the accompaniments European in flavor, the aisles wide and easy to navigate. Gleaming marble, brass and multi-colored glass dominate the scene. A one-story high Chihuly glass flower sculpture and two thousand smaller ones covered two thousand square feet of the lobby ceiling. The ever-changing conservatory and botanical gardens are exquisitely jaw dropping in splendor.

Yet, instead of being mesmerized by the colors and pomp, I ended up sitting at the edge of Bellagio's high limit slot room, watching a very unhappy woman wait for her six thousand dollars to be delivered by an attendant.

The ultra thin, and gold dripping female seemed irritated she had to wait until the win was validated before she could continue to gamble on the same machine. Her bird-leg like arms stretched out to the machine next to her and she slipped five one hundred dollar bills into the slot. The five bills didn't last long, not at the rate of fifty dollars a spin. Within a minute's time, she replaced the five hundred with another.

As I stood up to leave, I noticed a man being paid a thirty-four thousand dollar jackpot from playing a hundred dollar slot. I mouthed the word,

"Congratulations". He smirked back at me like I was an idiot. Thirty-four grand was nothing to be congratulated about, not in his world.

I enjoyed a bit of *schadenfreude* on my way to the tram, noting that he and I would more than likely end up at the same place at the end of the day … not a penny ahead and our money lost forever.

∞

It was late in the afternoon when I left the Monte Carlo. At one point my three hundred dollar stash for the day turned into seven hundred dollars. It took only a half hour of bad luck for my stack of bills to dwindle down to the original starting point. It was time to head to the Aria.

Straddling Las Vegas Boulevard and Harmon Avenue is the sixty-nine-acre City Center complex. The six gleaming glass high-rise towers present a dazzling and confusing site from the tram window. The size of the city within a city alone was perhaps the reason I would later become, as my grandmother would have said, discombobulated.

Two hours into gambling at the Aria, I still had money in my pocket, three hundred and twenty-two dollars to be exact. I was playing directly across from the Jean Philippe Patisserie, situated next to the North Valet station. Crème brule, rose macaroons, chocolate cheesecake, crepes covered with a mango and coconut sauce and an almond brioche called to me. The voices were so strong, I couldn't risk sitting near the shop another minute. It was time to leave by the nearest exit.

As soon as I stepped into the sunlight, I peered across an acre or more of elevated concrete, sitting high above Harmon Avenue. The elevated roundabout allowed for cars to be dropped off at the Aria's valet and traffic to pass underneath. The Vdara Hotel and Spa, sat on the other side.

In the center of the roundabout was Nancy Rubin's gigantic sculpture made of two hundred canoes and flat boats, held together by industrial strength guy-wire. The multi-colored watercraft were piled high and tilted upwards or sideways. The result was a vast bouquet of gleaming watercraft with not a lake in sight.

Rubin's work was fascinating to look at, but it didn't help me to head where I wanted to go. All I saw in front of me were buildings, and not a way down to the lower level which would lead me to Las Vegas Boulevard.

A bellman stopped in front of me for a breather as he struggled with a brass cart filled with Louis Vuitton luggage.

I asked him mid-grunt, "Can you tell me how to get to down to The Strip?"

He glanced me up and down before saying, "You want to go to the Bellagio?"

My ego got the best of me. *Wow, this guy thinks I'm classy!*

I nodded yes, though Bellagio was not on my radar. The polar opposite of an upscale casino, was my real destination, Circus Circus. The rest of my day was suppose to be spent with annoying clowns, trapeze artists who swung overhead, while I ate two-dollar hotdogs without the buns.

The bellman pointed toward Vdara. He said, "Go into the entrance directly across from us. Follow the signs and you'll end up at the back of Bellagio, right near the chocolate fountain."

Ah, ha! I didn't look like an elegant rich bitch after all. The bellman summed me up correctly. I was nothing more than a dedicated lover of all things chocolate.

Heading across the lot, I peered over the railing of the skywalk and watched cars and trucks whiz by underneath, delivering people and goods to the various buildings of the City Center Complex.

Reaching Vdara's doors, I made my first mistake. To the immediate right of the entrance, was an elevator with a plaque stating Harmon Avenue. An arrow pointed downward.

In the near distance to my east, I could see cars zipping along Las Vegas Boulevard. It would be so much closer to walk along Harmon Avenue. Plus, I could avoid walking by what I knew to be the world's largest chocolate fountain. I'd already had enough temptation for one day.

Instead of continuing on the recommended route, I decided to ride the elevator down to the lower level. When I reached the street, I noticed a sign featuring a stick figure man in full stride with a slant marked through him. The legendary "no pedestrian" sign. The next sign, right behind it, demanded a U-Turn be made immediately. Then there was yet another sign behind the second one, warning no access to Las Vegas Boulevard.

What do they mean, no access? I can see The Strip in front of me, I ranted. Two blocks away, max. The powers that be obviously wanted me to turn around, but that seemed silly and overly protective. And more than likely, they weren't as concerned about my safety as they were to urge me to walk through one casino after another, in hopes of my succumbing to gambling's spell.

I *certainly* wasn't going to fall for that old trick.

I bravely continued on, noticing the sidewalk getting slimmer, but it was still walk worthy, even when I could only manage to stay on it by placing one foot in front of the other. The only truly uncomfortable part was the cars whizzing by me, anxious to pull into the Cosmopolitan underground parking. The autos were only a few feet away, and getting closer by the minute as the sidewalk continued to narrow, and then, suddenly, the sidewalk ended.

Completely. Gone. Disappeared. History. The only remnant remaining was a five-inch concrete curb, resting against the steep elevated incline of rocks, earth, sand and cacti leaning against the building's vast wall.

Cars were beginning to honk non-stop, the drivers seeming unaware of my precarious situation. Streams of speeding motorists on one side of me, and an incline that I would not navigate on the other.

Las Vegas Boulevard was still a block away.

The smart thing to do would have been to turn around, but I couldn't. Every cell in my body revolted at turning my back to the traffic. Nor could I walk backwards, not with this body and my tendency to stumble even on the flattest and widest of surfaces. I had no choice but to move forward and plow ahead. Besides, there had to be some sort of an entry into the building along the way, I thought. There had to be.

There was, but every metal door was locked. I knew it would be useless to pound on them. There didn't appear to be a buzzer I could press either. Instead, I continued on, grabbing onto bushes and fauna to steady myself until finally, I was a mere twenty feet from The Strip.

But, there was no crosswalk, no stop sign, no way to cross The Strip. The traffic that turned on to the side street did it without benefit of a street signal.

I had no choice but to pull myself further up the incline, until I was finally at the top, standing behind a guardrail, on the opposite side of where I needed to be.

The sidewalk that runs across the front of the Cosmopolitan is elevated and is an estimated four feet off the ground. The chest high guardrail protects pedestrians from tumbling down the elevated slope, and into the traffic on Las Vegas Boulevard where they could easily be killed.

This was the situation as I described it later to a friend: Thousands of tourists were strolling nonchalantly down the sidewalk, a guard rail separating the walkers and me. However, I wasn't alone. A million cacti, palm trees and any other sticky and body invasive foliage the original landscapers could find surrounded me. Underneath my feet were small pebbles that, with every step I took rolled down the hill I found myself on, and into the traffic.

My terror was now two-fold. I was terrified I might slip and tumble downward, run over by the Deuce Express. Or that a cop would walk by at any minute. Jaywalking comes with a hefty fine in Las Vegas. The last I read, it was one hundred eighty dollars. Plus, I was destroying property with every step I took. Ripping off leaves, sending gravel into the stratosphere, kicking at cactus in anger when I felt a stabbing pain. I feared I would end up in jail just for being stupid.

So I continued to shuffle along the guardrail, hoping there was some gate in sight, or a place I could easily climb over the barricade. At my current weight, no one except a crew of fireman could lift me over the railing. And I certainly didn't have the strength to climb over it myself.

Instead, I held onto the guardrail tightly and moved crablike down the railing. This forced me to horizontally face the people passing by. Their faces were filled with looks of bemusement or a look that said, "Well, you're obviously homeless so you are invisible to me." I did manage to get a few chuckles when I said, "I kind of got lost" to people who bothered to ask what I was doing.

No one asked if they could help me.

I felt like an idiot. My legs were being continually cut by the cacti. My flimsy shirt snagged on palm trees. I could hear the material rip. When I came to the end of the railing, an entire block's worth of shuffling, I was overjoyed that there was an easy way for me to step around the railing and back onto the sidewalk. I was trembling as I did.

Continuing on to Circus Circus was now out of the question for me. All I wanted to do was hide out in my room until I stopped shaking.

Earlier that day I had hit a small jackpot of one hundred dollars. A man strolling by me at the time said, "You are one lucky lady."

He was right. I am lucky that my refusal to obey the obvious signs didn't turn out to be fatal. The only thing damaged was my pride.

Day Seven: Vegas

"What's the temperature at home?"

"Thirty-seven degrees, but it's going to warm up to forty-three," my husband answered.

Forty-three isn't a warm anything.

"Vegas?" he asked.

"Below normal, seventy-one degrees."

A mere one-degree below normal, but when you've traveled two thousand miles from the Northland you deserved every single degree.

"Call me from the train," he instructed.

"Yep," I answered. "Tomorrow morning, sometime."

In fourteen hours I would be leaving via an Amtrak shuttle to Kingman, Arizona. The van driver would be pulling out of McCarran International Airport at 10:00 p.m. It would be 1:30 a.m., or later, when I boarded the train and flopped into bed exhausted.

I hung around my hotel room longer than normal, checking email, taking time to write a decent five hundred words, reading another chapter in *Tracks*, calling a few friends. Before beginning or ending a journey, I feel a need to communicate to those I hold dear, the drama of a potential final farewell looming in the back of my mind.

I was still reeling from the previous day's cactus assault and sidewalk humiliation. Though I had made it to the last day, part of me was still convinced I'd keel over in Vegas, never to rise again. Or at least end up in

139

the hospital emergency room, my head filled with a million *I told you so's*.

After finishing my fond adieus to my buddies, I headed to the ATM machine for the last time. So far, my expenditures had been a worst-case scenario. Every possible penny was either lost in gambling or spent on buffets or fast food salads.

Shuffling through the maze at Paris, I gave a few hateful looks to the slots that hoovered my money the night before. I was being childish. It wasn't the machines fault that I'd acted like a fool, nor was it a conspiracy of the gambling gods dooming me to a life of perpetual loserdom.

It was just math. Period. Nothing more.

Reading, writing and arithmetic were never my strong points. Being dyslexic and brimming with learning disabilities in a period when such a diagnosis wasn't even on the horizon, I was never more than a C plus student. Being published at seventeen years of age didn't convince my high school English teacher that I was anything more than a weirdo who accidently, through no skill of her own, channeled a bit of talent from time to time.

Math was my particular downfall. Not only did the numbers appear backwards and upside down, my vision tended to be myopic. I could visualize only one number at a time.

I do the same thing now with the lottery. Most lottery players do. The phrase "Odds: 1 in 160 million" allows me to focus only on the "1". The one hundred sixty million assurances I would definitely not win a dime faded into the background.

So, it did not surprise me that although the odds were against it, I felt there was still a chance I'd redeem myself by the end of the day. If not on The Strip, then at the airport slots a few minutes before my scheduled departure.

The waters from the Bellagio fountain shimmered across the street. Traffic was picking up and the sidewalks were filling with bodies. At the last possible moment, I decided to board the slow moving Deuce and head north.

I was fortunate a woman in her 50s gave me her seat. From my perspective, she looked older than me. But then, on some days I think I look thirty, thirty-one tops. Winning at gambling isn't my only delusion.

One of my favorite comedy bits in my stand-up routine is when I tell the audience, "The last ten decades have been the happiest of my life. Want to know my secret?"

The crowd bleats out a resounding yes.

I respond, "Because ten years ago I stopped looking in the mirror."

That statement pretty much rings true for everyone, even the beautiful.

The bus is painstakingly slow. At every stop a passenger will board with a plastic container of booze in his hand, holding it proudly, knowing he can drink with ease on the streets of Las Vegas. The hawk-eyed driver will announce again that no drinks are allowed on board. The bus will wait an eternity until it dawns on the tipsy rider that the driver is talking about him. Sheepishly, the passenger will stumble off the bus to continue his drinking on the sidewalk.

I've yet to witness a drinker who chose riding over imbibing.

Thirty minutes of stops and halting starts later, I entered the Riviera for the last time. Two months earlier, the property was purchased by the Las Vegas Convention and Visitors Authority for a whopping one hundred and eighty-two million dollars. In a year or so, the one time glamorous and glitzy structure would be imploded, making way for a new convention center.

I've seen just about every movie in its entirety filmed at the Riviera: *Oceans 11, Casino, Showgirls, Austin Powers, The Hangover, 21, Vegas Vacation*, and *3,000 Miles to Graceland* were a delight. But, try as I might, I couldn't finish *Crazy Girls Undercover*. A low budget, B-movie combining terrorists and Vegas showgirls who worked on the side as CIA agents just didn't grab my attention. To be fair, eighteen percent of the viewers on Rotten Tomatoes did give it a thumbs-up.

For over a quarter of a century, the Crazy Girls bared breasts and buns in a dance revue that originated at the Riviera. I witnessed the erotic extravaganza only once, but I've never forgotten it. I've never laughed as hard in my life as I did that night.

Oklahoma is one of my favorite Rodgers and Hammerstein musicals. In high school, I proudly wore a simple farm girl dress and stood in the chorus, singing loudly in virginal innocence. Even with my vast and often sordid imagination, I could not have dreamt that decades later, a silicone enhanced, topless bimbo would burst onto the stage in front of me, lip syncing my favorite song from the musical, *I'm Just a Girl Who Can't Say No*. Her mini-skirt and thong made of the same red and white checkered gingham as my onstage prairie dress.

Our breasts and buns, however, had nothing in common.

I've had a soft spot in my heart for the Riviera ever since, and it was no wonder I wanted to say goodbye to it. A dozen people were scattered around, sad looks on their faces, their hands pressing buttons while their other hand picked up a cocktail.

Struggling to breathe normally, I plopped in front of a penny slot. The older casinos were built with low ceilings that capture cigarette smoke and send it swirling back downwards to form clouds that circled my head.

"Would you care for a drink? Bloody Mary? Screwdriver? Whiskey?" the aging cocktail waitress offered.

"Just water," I answered and tipped her two bucks for the bottle. From the looks of her, she was hired the day the Riviera opened in 1955.

I played for a few hours, managing to leave eighty dollars as a memorial. During my entire stay at the Riviera, I didn't hear a single jackpot being won, or a whoop of happiness streaming across the room.

Joy had left the building.

∞

Directly across the street from the Riviera, a one hundred and seventy-three foot neon Jester welcomed me as I entered Circus Circus. I wasn't "stoned, ripped and twisted", like Hunter S. Thompson was when he wrote his masterpiece, *Fear and Loathing in Las Vegas*. If I had been, I might have walked out. The atmosphere hardly needed drugs to enhance or exaggerate it, though they might help to describe it.

Billed as family friendly and fun-for-all the casino is a kitschy mixture of cheap Barnum and Baily extravaganzas, rundown county fair midways with questionable carney workers and budget-minded gamblers rolled into one big appetizer and spread across a worn, ugly multi-color carpet of reds, greens and dust. Kids and family are everywhere, running to view the free circus acts presented throughout the day.

High in the air, a Ukrainian dancer dangled, a silk scarf wrapped around her body the only means of support. A stunningly beautiful female Asian foot juggler laid back on two wooden chairs swirling brightly colored parasols with her feet. A family of South American trapeze artists leapt from platform to platform. And then there were the clowns, friendly, scary, real, and even, at times, plastic.

143

Slot machines are positioned on revolving carousel platforms, reminiscent of the amusement park ride I loved as a kid. Brand, spanking new automobiles are set high above slot machines with posters on all sides declaring, "Win This Car."

A few hours into play, and after I'd given up on winning a silver Ford Taurus, I ended up seated next to an older woman at a dollar slot machine. A look of confusion displayed on her face, she kept mumbling, "Damn it, the machine's broken."

I looked over and saw three sevens lined up. Yet, she continued to pull at the lever. Unknowingly, she'd just won one-thousand dollars.

"It won't spin," she told a slot attendant who stepped up to her side. "I think I broke it."

His response was to nod his head, and mumble back, "Broke it?"

She nodded.

"Okay," he said, reaching over to open the door of the machine, in order to "fix it."

What the hell! I'd never seen that happen in a casino, though I'd heard rumors that it did. In my eyes, the slot attendant appeared to be trying to con her out of a win. Once the machine door was opened, and the inner workings were reset, her thousand-dollar win would be invalidated – though she didn't know she won it in the first place.

I reached over and touched the lady's forearm, and said, "It isn't broken. You've won a thousand bucks. That's what those three sevens mean. That's why the light is flashing on top."

She looked up at the spinning beams before asking the slot attendant, "Really?"

He stood silent, as if I would retract my statement and admit I was wrong.

In a louder and more irritated tone, I said. "She *won* a jackpot."

He grumbled, "Oh yeah, I see that now. I'll get someone to pay her."

"Thanks," the woman said to me, still somewhat in shock over her good fortune.

"No problem," I answered, livid in my assumption the employee had tried to rip her off by agreeing the machine was broken. Whether his actions were casino supported or just his own little power trip, I had no idea.

I remained there until I made sure the woman was paid her due. By the time ten, one hundred dollar bills where placed in her outstretched palm, I was down to sixty bucks. It was time to head back to my hotel and pack.

No big deal, I decided as I sat on the Deuce, watching The Strip zip by me. There was still a chance to win all of my money back, the entire two thousand sixty dollars for the week. And, I'd do it right before I left town, at the airport.

It could happen.

It has happened.

So, why not happen to me?

∞

On February 27th a mere five weeks before I pathetically stood in front of an airport slot hoping to win back a week's worth of wagers, a $300,499.30 jackpot on a Wheel of Fortune machine was awarded to a lucky traveler at McCarran International Airport. The win, though a life changing amount in my eyes, didn't even make the papers, the dollar amount too trivial to report by Vegas standards.

Over thirteen hundred slot machines are situated around the Las Vegas airport. Online trolls warn the slots are notoriously tight. According to a much dated survey on the website wizardofodds.com (some of the data going back as far as 2001) McCarran's payback is at the bottom of the list. There are seventy-one casinos listed and McCarran's payback was reported to be

81.2%. The Palms casino was the highest at 93.42%. The Strip, where I lost most of my cash, ranked in the 91% ballpark, give or take a few decimals.

Even knowing the statistics were not in my favor, I always keep sixty dollars in my pocket to gamble at McCarran. It's not that I think I will win, I won't. Of that I am pretty certain, but I am enthralled with the possibility of a story—the one I could tell my friends.

"It was three minutes before I was scheduled to leave Las Vegas. I was down to my last dollar when suddenly three red sevens lined up in front of me. The jackpot amount was staggering. I won..."

Yada

Yada

Yada

I have done many things in my life I wished I hadn't. After making life altering mistakes, I'd rationalize that someday I would write about the mistakes, and that would make it all better. I truly believed scribbling down words would help me to be forgiven, or at least understood. Growing up in a fundamentalist family, confessing your sins, and seeking redemption were always the elephants in the room. They were the promised elixir for all things sinful, or human.

So it was easy to understand why, in the airport's baggage claim area, I sat at a slot, once again pondering. The trip to Las Vegas had been taxing, physically and emotionally. It had also been expensive, but not more so than a week at a fancy spa resort or renting a cabin in Northern Minnesota. I had fun of sorts, but then I always had a limited amount of fun wherever I go. I usually don't have to travel two thousand miles one way to achieve that.

My actual amount of time spent gambling probably averaged four or five hours a day. The rest of the time was spent getting to and from slowly, or recuperating from the effort. Every evening I was in my room by 6:00 p.m. If there is a sin connected to my trip, it certainly was that one.

Who goes to their room at 6:00 p.m. in Vegas? And spends the evening alone?

Old, tired, sick and broke people, a pathetic trifecta in which I was a member.

But, still, as I sat in my room at night, I could look out and see a million lights glitter, watch pedestrians on the street still filled with excitement at living. I'd reached the age where I was living a shadow life—barely noticeable by those who still danced in the sun.

It was obvious I was too old, too ill, and too disabled to be in Las Vegas anymore. It was time to go home, this time for good.

Goodbye, Sin City.

Unless, of course, I somehow managed to beat the odds and stopped my health, disabilities, and finances from declining at a rapid speed.

I am a gambler after all.

And, I have to believe in something. Most people do. A stroke of luck seems as likely as anything. There was a miniscule chance I would be able to come back to Vegas, one day.

I believe in chances, even the second or the one-hundredth one. If I didn't believe, then why have I ended up standing in front of an airport slot with my last five dollars in hand, hoping, praying, that at the last minute before boarding the Amtrak shuttle I will finally, miraculously, and against all odds...

END

About the Author

Pat Dennis is the award-winning author of *Hotdish To Die For*, a collection of six mystery short stories where the weapon of choice is hotdish, deadly recipes included. Readers demanding more were rewarded with *Hotdish Haiku*, featuring 50 haiku and recipes from her and other writers. *Murder by Chance* is the first of her Betty Chance Mysteries series. The second, *Killed by Chance*. The third Betty Chance Mystery book is planned to follow soon after.

Pat's short stories and humor appear in many anthologies, including Anne Frasier's *Deadly Treats; Who Died in Here?; The Silence of the Loons: Resort to Murder; Fifteen tales of Murder, Mayhem and Malice From the Land of Minnesota Nice*; *Once Upon a Crime Anthology*; *Writes of Spring*; and *Mood Change*. She is the author of the novel *Stand-Up and Die. The Witches of Dorkdom*, a middle school fantasy and mystery novel was published under her pseudonym, Nora England. Pat performed as a stand-up comedian with over 1,000 performances at comedy clubs, Fortune 500 companies, Women's Expos, and special events. She has appeared on the same venue as Lewis Black, Phyllis Diller, and David Brenner. Visit her at www.patdennis.com. For recipes, contests and restaurant reviews visit Pat and her alter ego "Betty Chance" at www.buffetbetty.com.

Books by Pat Dennis

Murder by Chance
Killed by Chance
Hotdish To Die For
Fat Old Woman in Las Vegas:
  Gambling, Dieting & Wicked Fun
Stand-Up and Die
Mood Change and other stories
Who Died in Here?
Hotdish Haiku

BOOKS WRITTEN AS NORA ENGLAND

The Witches of Dorkdom

ANTHOLOGIES / PAT DENNIS
Anne Frasier's *Deadly Treats*
The Silence of the Loons
Resort to Murder
Fifteen Tales of Murder, Mayhem and Malice
Once Upon A Crime Anthology
Writes of Spring
Cooked To Death (Fall 2016)

Acknowledgments

Thank you to Marilyn Victor, my exceptional editor and good friend. A shout out to Rhonda Gilliand, my favorite beta reader and bud. To Donna Seline, owner of Typesetting a la Macque, who so far has been the only woman brave enough to not only travel to Las Vegas with me, but is kind enough to allow me to use the photo she took of me winning a jackpot. My continued gratitude to Theresa Weir (AKA Anne Frasier) for your support and believing in this project. No one could ask for better friends than I have. And to the online writers group that welcomes me as a member. I only finished this book because I told you I would.

Made in the USA
Charleston, SC
22 April 2016